THE
ENTREPRENEUR'S
TICKETS

A STEP-BY-STEP GUIDE

TO BUILDING YOUR DREAM BUSINESS

OMARY S. OMARY

Published by Tax Digital Lamp

First Edition

ISBN 978-9912-42-253-7 (Paperback)

ISBN 978-9912-42-254-4 (E-Book)

ISBN 979-8303-00-050-6 (Hardcover)

Printed in the United States of America

Dedication

This book is for every aspiring entrepreneur in Tanzania and around the world. Your dreams matter, and your hard work can transform your life and your community. I hope this guide inspires you to follow your passion and build the business you've always imagined.

Acknowledgments

First and foremost, I want to thank God for giving me the strength and guidance to complete this book.

I am deeply grateful to my wife, Barke J. Baghozah, and my child, Maahad O. Seif, for their unwavering patience and support throughout this journey. Your love and encouragement have been my greatest source of inspiration.

I also want to extend my thanks to my friends and everyone who has supported me along the way. Your belief in me helped make this book possible.

Finally, to the readers, thank you for allowing me to be a part of your journey. I hope this book helps you take meaningful steps toward building your dream.

Table of Content

Introduction

With over six years of experience providing consulting services to entrepreneurs, I've had the opportunity to work with clients from all corners of the world, including the USA, UK, Canada, UAE, China, and my beloved home, Tanzania. Along this journey, I've seen that people from different cultures and backgrounds share the same dream: building something big. Yet, many of them also share the same hurdles, like feeling stuck, unsure of where to start, what steps to take, or how to overcome challenges.

This is what motivated me to write this book. I am excited to welcome you to *The Entrepreneur's Tickets: A Step-by-Step Guide to Building Your Dream Business!*

This book is not just a bunch of words; it is your guide, friend, and map to help you step by step on your journey to becoming an entrepreneur. Whether you are thinking of starting a business or are already on the path, this book will support you every step of the way.

This book shows you that anyone can officially begin their entrepreneurial journey. It doesn't matter if you're starting small, have limited resources, or have never run a business before. With this book in your hand and the right mindset, you can build a successful venture!

What This Book Offers

As you begin your journey into the world of entrepreneurship, think of this book as a set of special tickets that enable you to go to your desired destination. Each ticket will bring you closer to your dream of owning a successful business.

With the first ticket, we'll explore the starting point of your journey. This is where everything begins. You'll learn how to take those important first steps into entrepreneurship, discover what motivates you, and choose a business idea that excites you. It's not just about picking any idea; it's about finding one that matches your skills and passions. Once you've got that idea, we'll work on creating a business plan that outlines your vision, goals, and the steps you need to take. Just as you wouldn't go on a trip without knowing your destination, you need a plan to guide your business journey. This part will help you set clear goals and a path to follow.

Also, we'll focus on gathering the resources you need to succeed and finding the perfect location for your business. Resources include everything from the right people to the tools and materials that will help your business run smoothly. We'll also talk about how to choose a location, whether it's a physical store, an office, or an online space. The place you choose will have a big impact on how your business attracts customers and how it operates. You'll learn how to pick a location that fits your needs and draws in the right people.

Now, the second ticket will guide you through the legal steps needed to start your business. This is where you learn how to officially register your business, get the right tax documents, and secure your business license. This ticket ensures you have all the necessary permits to operate smoothly. Without them, you could face problems that might slow you down. When your business is set up properly, you'll have peace of mind and be able to focus on growth without worrying about legal issues.

Finally, the third ticket is where things get interesting! It's time to share your business with the world and officially launch it. We'll focus on branding, which helps create a unique identity for your business that connects with customers. We'll also cover marketing, which is how to spread the word and attract your audience. You'll learn how to reach people and make them interested in what you're offering.

But we won't stop there! After branding and marketing, it's time to launch your business. Launching means starting your operations and opening your doors, whether online or in a physical space. This is the moment to welcome your first customer. You'll learn how to prepare for this moment, ensuring everything is set for a smooth and successful launch. We'll guide you step by step, so you'll feel confident and ready when the time comes to share your business with the world.

After each lesson in every ticket of the book, you'll have a chance to reflect on your journey with self-assessment questions. These questions will help you evaluate your progress and focus on what steps you need to take next. They'll serve as checkpoints, keeping you aligned with your vision as you move forward.

By the end of this journey, you'll have all the knowledge and tools you need to confidently build your dream business. You'll be ready to turn your ideas into something big, a business that reflects your hard work and passion.

Let's Get Started!

Take a moment to find some calm. Let your thoughts settle. Now, think about where you could be a year from now. What do you see? Maybe you have your own business, full of customers. Perhaps you're offering products or services that people love and share with others. That bright future is closer than you think, and this book will help you reach it. All it takes is a willingness to learn, a commitment to take action, and a belief in yourself.

Think about the pride you will feel as your hard work begins to bear fruit. consider the relationships you'll build with your customers, the joy of watching them enjoy what you provide, and the thrill of achieving your goals. This book will lead you to that pride.

After all, by choosing to read this book, you've already taken an important step on this journey. Yes, there will be moments that challenge you, but with the information and encouragement you'll find here, you'll be ready to face anything that comes your way.

So, are you ready to begin this journey together?

Let's go!

Ticket 1

Starting Your Journey

First Step

"The journey of a thousand miles begins with one step."

— Lao Tzu

If you want to be an entrepreneur but find yourself hesitating to take even the smallest action, you might not yet have what it takes to be successful. This affects your progress, confidence, and motivation.

If you let questions like, "Am I ready for this journey?" consume your mind, you're making a big mistake. Stop that! This keeps you stuck and makes you miss out on big opportunities.

In this chapter, you'll get simple tips to guide you through the early stages of entrepreneurship, reflect on your journey, and pursue the success you've always dreamed about. If doubts or feeling stuck have been your co-pilot, this chapter will help you kick them out and take the driver's seat with a confident first step!

Big Thing

Success is a dream you hold close to your heart, isn't it? If you're nodding, I completely understand; it's a feeling many of us share. Let's go back a few years to my days as an undergraduate student. I remember sitting with friends and asking them one by one, "What does success mean to you?" Expecting the usual answers about careers or big goals, I was in for a surprise!

One friend boldly declared that success meant owning a Lamborghini by the age of 25 and earning respect from everyone around him. He insisted that if he didn't have one by then, he'd consider himself a total failure. Another friend's dream had us all laughing; success, to her, was marrying a top African celebrity, Diamond Platnumz. She pictured herself walking down red carpets, waving at fans, and trying to decide whether to call him "Honey" or "Darling" in public!

Then there was the friend who believed success was a big monthly salary that would ease all life's worries, plus a fridge full of ice cream. He laughed and said, "If I can binge-watch movies and eat ice cream whenever I want, then I'll know I've made it!"

Their answers showed me how success means something different to everyone, and while I don't dismiss that, it can be a wonderful definition for them.

But let's go beyond that. True success is about building something bigger, your own big thing that leaves a lasting impact. This "big thing" could be a business that provides jobs and valuable products or services to people, or it might be a big idea that inspires others and continues to make a difference long after you're gone. Success, in this way, becomes more than just a personal dream; it's a gift to the world, one that fills you with pride, knowing you've built a legacy.

But how do you reach that level? The journey begins with taking your first step into the world of entrepreneurship. You might be wondering, "How do I take that first step?"

It all starts with identifying new solutions to problems around you and following your dream of building something of your own. By doing this, you open the door to becoming one of the world's successful entrepreneurs.

Even if you choose to start small, what truly matters is taking that first step. Every journey begins with a single action. That initial step leads to another, and then another. Before you know it, you'll look back and realize you've built something much bigger and truly remarkable.

Always remember that if you keep sleeping, you'll only dream about success without ever turning it into a reality. So, I urge you to wake up! Stop waiting for someone to shake you awake and push you to transform your aspirations into achievements. What if no one comes? No one else can take that first step for you. It's your own success, and it's up to you to make it happen.

Fear is Your Death

When you allow fear to control your choices, it's like letting a death of the bright future you could create. You miss out on the chances that could help you live the dream you've always wanted. I understand that feeling afraid is a natural part of being human. Everyone faces fear, especially when trying something new. Even successful people you admire, like Mark Zuckerberg, Warren Buffett, and Steve Jobs, felt the same fear before they began their remarkable journeys.

Facing your fear to start your big thing can be difficult, but it's definitely worth it. Look at successful entrepreneurs like Oprah Winfrey. She didn't wait for fear to disappear before starting. Growing up in poverty, she faced many challenges but refused to let them hold her back. Instead of thinking, "I come from a poor background; I can't succeed," she recognized the chance to make her dream happen and embraced it. Today, she is celebrated not only as a powerful media figure but also for her remarkable accomplishments as a television host, actress, producer, and philanthropist.

The success of Oprah illustrates that you shouldn't let your fear be your death; instead, it should be your birth of the success you truly desire. When it comes to failure, think of it as a tool to help you learn again and again so you can grow and improve.

Many successful entrepreneurs didn't run away from failure; they welcomed it as part of their journey. Each time they fell, they discovered something new and valuable that helped them get back up, stronger than before. So, don't be afraid of failure. Instead, be afraid of standing still, of letting fear keep you from reaching your full potential. Embrace the lessons that come from falling and use them to fuel your progress toward achieving your dreams.

Embrace Your Own Dream

Look at the world we live in today. If someone like Steve Jobs had chosen to ignore his dream, would we have iPhones in our hands? Instead of sticking to a secure job with a comfortable salary, he chased his own big thing. Because of that choice, we now have a device that transformed how we connect with each other.

Look, sometimes you may hold a golden ticket for a special journey, one that could lead you to a future where your dreams become reality. But instead of using that ticket, you choose to stay behind, investing your time and energy into someone else's vision. Each day, you pour your talents into building another person's big thing, while your own dreams slowly fade away.

This happens to many people. They settle into jobs where they feel secure, comforted by the promise of a monthly paycheck. It's easy to stay in a job where you feel safe, but think about this: what if you spend your whole life helping someone else succeed while your own dreams remain unfulfilled? It's normal to feel scared about leaving a good job. Yes, it is risky. But the bigger risk is staying in a place where your dreams never have a chance to be realized.

Maybe you are waiting for a perfect moment to take that step, a time when you'll have more experience, more resources, or a better plan. Maybe you tell yourself, "When things are better, then I'll start."

If this sounds familiar, the reality is that the perfect time to move toward your dreams may never come. Waiting for everything to fall into place might mean missing opportunities that could change your life. Life is unpredictable, and the perfect time rarely exists.

Sometimes, taking that first step into the world of entrepreneurship when things aren't ideal is the best choice you can make. Starting in challenging times teaches you lessons that make you strong. You become resilient, resourceful, and able to face challenges head-on. Those early struggles may seem scary, but they prepare you for success. You learn how to survive, how to think creatively, and how to keep going even when it feels like the world is against you.

Understand Your Journey

Before stepping into the world of entrepreneurship, let's take a few minutes to understand what this journey truly means. Many people think being an entrepreneur is solely about making profits. Sure, who wouldn't love a fancy house or a luxurious life? But the truth is, starting in entrepreneurship means you're stepping into a world of risks and challenges that can make your journey to success both exciting and scary, while also creating meaningful changes that can help the world.

But know that taking risks is a big part of this journey. So, being ready to step onto this path means you're willing to try new things, even if you're not sure how they will turn out. While making profits is important, focusing solely on that goal might cause you to miss the bigger picture. True success as an entrepreneur is about helping those around you. For example, when you hire your first employee, you are helping them by giving them a job. If your business solves a problem for someone, even if they are far away in another country, you are making a difference in their life.

Also, let's clear something up: entrepreneurs aren't born; they're made. Some folks might think that being a successful entrepreneur requires some special, hidden talent or skills, but honestly, they're just kidding themselves. The truth is, anyone can become an entrepreneur! It's not a gift you're born with; it's something you can develop through experience.

Every successful entrepreneur has faced doubts and challenges. What sets them apart is their willingness to learn, adapt, and keep moving forward. It's true that some, like Elon Musk, may seem like natural-born entrepreneurs, but their success is actually the result of dedication and hard work. They've made mistakes, taken risks, and learned valuable lessons along the way.

Also, understand that entrepreneurship is a mindset, not some secret formula or hidden magical tool you're born with. It's about waking up every day with the mindset to solve problems, improve, and make a difference, while holding onto the motivation to keep going even when things get tough. It's like being a detective, always on the lookout for problems to solve and ways to do things better, on your own terms.

After all, if you've ever thought, "OMG, being an entrepreneur is way harder than I thought! Maybe I wasn't meant to be a CEO," just remember that even the best CEOs didn't start with a perfect plan. They began right where you are now. With time and effort, you can start your entrepreneurial journey and become the CEO of your own business. In other words, you don't need to be born with a briefcase in hand; you can earn it step by step and proudly go from "I can't" to "I did!"

Entrepreneurs vs. Businesspeople

While all entrepreneurs are businesspeople, not all businesspeople are entrepreneurs. Both start and run businesses, but their approaches often differ. Have you ever thought about what sets them apart? Understanding their differences can help you on your own path to success.

One way entrepreneurs stand out is in how they approach business ideas. They have a passion for creating something new and unique, aiming to lead rather than just follow. Take Idrisa Bozen, for instance. He dreams of opening a milk shop, but if he only sells the same milk as everyone else, he's just another businessperson. While he'd be part of the market, he'd lack a unique touch.

Then, Idrisa sees an opportunity: people in his town are looking for fresh, high-quality organic milk. He decides to offer this special product, creating a shop that truly stands out. Idrisa even organizes community events to share the health benefits of organic milk, bringing people together and educating them on nutrition. By doing so, he doesn't just run a milk shop; he becomes an entrepreneur who adds real value to his community, inspiring others. This ability to create unique ideas is what truly sets entrepreneurs apart.

Many entrepreneurs have two main aims: to make a profit and to help others. They aspire to make the world a better place through their businesses. Idrisa reflects this spirit; his milk shop doesn't just sell organic milk, it also educates the community about healthier choices. By providing a product they can trust, Idrisa creates a sense of pride and connection in the community, showing how entrepreneurs can create positive change in the world around them.

On the other hand, businesspeople often focus primarily on profit. They aim to make money and maintain their business, but they may not prioritize helping others or making a positive impact. Their main goal is usually to compete in the market and ensure that their business is successful financially. While this is important, it can sometimes lead them to follow trends rather than create new ones.

How entrepreneurs handle risk is also essential. They are willing to take smart risks and understand that failure is part of the journey. Instead of fearing mistakes, they view them as chances to learn and grow. When Idrisa invests his time and money in his organic milk shop, he knows he's taking a risk. His creative idea might not work out, but he believes in his dream and is ready to give it a shot. Although stepping into new territory can be challenging, Idrisa understands that every step, whether successful or not, is part of his meaningful journey. In contrast, a typical businessperson might hesitate to take such risks.

I believe you now have a clearer understanding of entrepreneurs and businesspeople, which will help you shape your own journey. Embrace your creativity, aim for meaningful goals, and don't shy away from taking smart risks.

Key Qualities to Help You Succeed

Becoming an entrepreneur isn't only about starting a business or having a great idea; it's about enjoying the journey and developing the important qualities that help you succeed. One key quality for any entrepreneur is perceptiveness. This means you can see opportunities where others see problems. This skill helps you find ways to succeed when things seem unclear, and everyone else is ready to give up.

Next is the ability to take risks. This doesn't mean jumping off a cliff without a parachute, that's just asking for trouble! Taking risks means having the courage to follow your dreams, even when you're not sure what will happen. Often, real success comes from stepping into the unknown and saying, "Let's see where this unpredictable road leads!" It's like welcoming the future with open arms; you might find something amazing or at least a funny story to tell later!

Ambition is the fuel that keeps your entrepreneurial engine running. It's that powerful inner push that drives you to work hard every day to make your dream real. Even when the journey is difficult, there's a voice inside you shouting, "You can do it!" This reminds you that you're reaching for something bigger and keeps you focused on what truly matters.

Creative thinking is where the fun really begins. It's all about coming up with new ideas and looking at problems in different ways. When you think creatively, you can turn a big mess into something wonderful. For example, while someone else might see a roadblock, you might see an opportunity to build a bridge over it, even painting it with bright colors to make it stand out. This is the magic of creative thinking. It keeps your business exciting and makes every day feel like a new adventure, where every obstacle becomes a fresh opportunity to shine.

Innovation works hand in hand with creativity by taking those creative ideas and turning them into practical, useful, and impactful solutions that can work in the real world. It helps you stay competitive and adapt to new trends in your industry. Innovation allows you to approach problems in different ways, setting you apart from others.

Decisiveness is key, too! It means you don't waste time thinking endlessly. Instead, you gather the facts, make a choice, and take action, saying, "Let's go for it!" Being decisive helps you grab opportunities like they're the last piece of delicious cake that you can't let slip by!

And then there's passion; it's the energy that drives every entrepreneur. It fuels your success and energizes your work. When you love what you do, it shows in your efforts. Passion motivates you to keep going, even during tough times, and it inspires others to believe in your vision. When you're passionate, you enjoy the process, feel connected to your business, and feel proud of what you're achieving. It's this passion that keeps you engaged and focused on your goals.

As an entrepreneur, embracing resilience is crucial. Resilience is the strength to stay strong when life throws challenges your way and to keep going when obstacles appear. It's normal to feel disappointed or frustrated when things go wrong. But resilience is what helps you get back up, brush off the dust, and say, "Well, that was unexpected! Let's try again!" It gives you the strength to keep moving forward, adjust your approach, and stay focused on your goals.

Success isn't about having just one special quality; it's a mix of many qualities: perceptiveness, risk-taking, ambition, creativity, innovation, self-confidence, decisiveness, passion, and resilience. By building these qualities, you'll not only reach your entrepreneurial dreams but also inspire others along the way.

Your Mindset

If you're like many people who want to create something meaningful, you may wonder what it truly takes to succeed in entrepreneurship. One of the most important aspects is having the right mindset. As entrepreneur, your mindset involves how you think, how you tackle challenges, and how you recognize opportunities. Your mindset is shaped by what you know, what you believe, and your attitudes, which all guide your choices in the business world. It can either support or hinder your progress, so it's essential to choose the right one to achieve success. Each choice can lead you down a different path, so consider carefully which mindset resonates with you most.

There's something called *a fixed mindset*. If you have this mindset, you believe your skills and abilities are difficult to change and reshape, like a big stone in that can never ever be broken. You might feel pressure to always prove yourself, leading you to avoid challenges for fear that mistakes will make you look weak. Assume you're starting a small popcorn stall. In the beginning, things don't go well, and some customers don't enjoy the taste. Instead of taking their feedback as a valuable insight, you feel embarrassed and think, "Maybe I'm just not good at this."

This reaction leads you to focus on the negative. You might think about how others are judging your popcorn or how you're failing to meet their expectations. Instead of experimenting with new flavors or adjusting your recipe, you decide to give up altogether, convinced that you can't improve. You miss out on the chance to ask your customers what they liked or didn't like, which could help you make necessary changes. This fear of failure stops you from trying new ideas or seeking support from fellow entrepreneurs. You close yourself off from feedback and learning opportunities, limiting your growth. Many people with a fixed mindset hide their struggles and abandon their dreams, worried about failing in front of others. They let that initial setback define their journey, missing the joy that comes from persistence and the valuable lessons that arise from each challenge.

Now, let's move to another way of thinking: *the growth mindset.* With this mindset, you believe you can improve through practice and hard work. Challenges become exciting chances to learn, and feedback is seen as helpful, not hurtful. View yourself as running the same popcorn stall, but this time with a growth mindset. When customers give feedback, you greet it with open arms, seeing it as an opportunity for growth. You ask them what they like and how you can do better, turning their opinions into stepping stones for success.

You might even take a cooking class or experiment with new recipes based on what you learned from your customers. This willingness to adapt and grow means that over time, your popcorn becomes tastier and more creative, attracting a loyal group of customers who can't wait to try your latest creations. As your skills improve, you share your journey online, talking about your mistakes and how you worked to fix them. This honesty not only builds trust with your customers but also creates a supportive community. People feel inspired by your resilience, encouraging them to keep trying, even when things get tough.

This mindset is what sets successful entrepreneurs apart from those who are afraid to take risks. Rather than running away from challenges, they embrace them, knowing that each experience contributes to their growth.

This mindset is what sets successful entrepreneurs apart from those who are afraid to take risks. Instead of running away from problems, it acts as your guiding light on the path to building your business. This mindset supports you in becoming the person you want to be.

Developing the Right Mindset

So, how can I develop a successful entrepreneurial mindset? You might ask yourself this question, and while it may seem daunting, it's easier than you think. Building this mindset doesn't require anything extraordinary; it simply requires embracing a growth mindset and committing to continuous personal development. This involves actively seeking out new experiences, learning from failures, and being open to feedback.

Surrounding yourself with like-minded individuals who share your ambitions can further enhance your mindset. Engage with mentors who can provide guidance, and participate in networking opportunities that expose you to different perspectives. This supportive environment will encourage you to take calculated risks and help you navigate the ups and downs of your entrepreneurial journey.

Practice self-reflection regularly. Ask yourself what you've learned from each experience, how you can apply those lessons, and what new skills you can develop. This proactive approach will empower you to adapt to changes in the market and ensure that your business remains relevant and competitive. Remember, entrepreneurs don't just follow the market; they actively shape it with their new ideas, skills, and creativity.

When you actively build a growth mindset, you will not only enhance your own capabilities but also create a positive atmosphere within your business. This mindset will help you inspire your team, engage your customers, and ultimately lead to greater success in your entrepreneurial endeavors.

Your Self-Discovery

Since you are about to finish this chapter, take a moment to ask yourself a simple but important question: Who are you? This isn't just about your name or your job. It's about looking inside yourself to find the qualities, values, and beliefs that guide your choices. When you know yourself better, your goals can match your actions. This way, the business you create shows your true passions and strengths. Think of it like painting a picture, every brushstroke represents a part of you.

Think about what you are good at. What skills make you stand out? Many successful entrepreneurs use their strengths to create value. Are you creative, a good problem-solver, or a natural leader? Knowing your strengths helps you find where you can shine and make a difference.

It's also important to think about your weaknesses. Everyone has them, and recognizing where you struggle is a key step to growing. Are there skills you want to improve or habits you want to change? Being honest about your weaknesses lets you plan how to overcome them, whether by learning new skills or finding the right people to support you.

Your values are very important. What principles guide your choices? What causes do you care about? The best businesses reflect the personal beliefs of the person behind them. Whether it's honesty, creativity, or helping others, knowing what you stand for will shape not just your business but also how you run it.

Now, think about your motivations. Why do you want to be an entrepreneur? Is it to achieve financial freedom, make a positive impact, or build something you truly love? Your "why" will push you forward. When challenges come, and they will, understanding your purpose will help you keep going.

Self-Reflection

Take a moment with the small task below. It will help you see how you fit into this journey before starting the next chapter.

Questions	My Answer
1. What does success mean to me?	
2. Can I think of a time when fear held me back?	
3. What is my "big thing" that I want to achieve?	
4. How do I feel about taking risks in my journey?	
5. Who are some entrepreneurs I admire and why?	
6. What qualities do I think are essential for success?	
7. Do I have a fixed or growth mindset?	
- If fixed, what beliefs limit my potential?	
- If growth, how do I embrace challenges?	
8. How do I plan to overcome my weaknesses?	
9. What motivates me to pursue my entrepreneurial goals?	
10. What steps will I take toward entrepreneurship?	

Figure 1.1: Self-Assessment Questions

Chapter 2

Creating Your Business Idea

"You can't just sit there and wait for people to give you that golden opportunity. You have to create it."

— Chris Gardner

Once you make the choice to take the first step toward becoming an entrepreneur, you'll realize that you need a solid business idea to accompany your journey. This is where the process of creating that idea comes into play.

In this chapter, you'll discover how to create your winning business idea and explore key questions to guide your journey. You'll learn which ideas to avoid, helping you stay focused, realistic, and on the right track.

To make things even easier, you'll be introduced to 135 top business ideas, giving you plenty of inspiration to choose from. Plus, you'll have the chance to conduct a self-assessment.

Business Idea

I believe that every entrepreneur with a successful mindset views a business idea as a hidden treasure, just waiting to be discovered. This treasure is filled with shining coins that represent wonderful opportunities. Each coin symbolizes a chance to make a difference, to solve a problem, or to bring something valuable into people's lives.

You can probably agree with me that a business idea is a dream aimed at solving a problem or offering something new to the world. It often begins with a simple question: "What if I try this?" This question opens the door to a world of possibilities that can change your life and create the foundation for a successful business.

As you explore your idea, you'll feel the joy of finding ways to help others and make their lives better, bringing smiles and hope along the way. In those moments, you'll experience a sense of happiness, purpose, and pride growing inside you. "This is the power of a business idea," you'll think, feeling proud of the endless possibilities it brings.

While a business idea may seem like just a possibility in its early stages, much like any other dream, it is the foundation of every successful company you know in the world. You might be surprised to learn that it can be something simple, like a way to make daily tasks easier, or something ambitious, like a technology that changes lives. But it is truly the unique value that has the power to change the world. After all, as you start your entrepreneurial journey, consider what sets your idea apart and how it can truly shine in the marketplace.

Many people believe they need to invent something entirely new to make their idea shine or stand out in the market for easy success. But here's the good news: that's not always true. Sometimes, success comes from taking an existing idea and discovering ways to make it better. So, don't worry if your idea is inspired by something familiar; what truly matters is the special touch you bring to it.

Look at Aliko Dangote, the richest entrepreneur in Africa. He didn't invent cement or sugar, but he changed how the cement and sugar industries worked in Africa by improving production methods and streamlining distribution. His journey teaches us that you can achieve great success by not just inventing something new. It's about seeing what others might miss and finding a way to make it better. With determination and creative thinking, Dangote built a remarkable empire that impacts lives and economies.

Diamond Platnumz, a famous musician and entrepreneur from Tanzania, is another good example. He didn't create Tanzania music, but he brought it to a global audience, especially through the Bongo Fleva genre. By blending different styles, including R&B, hip-hop, and traditional African sounds, he made his music unique and appealing.

His dance moves are just as captivating as his music; they combine traditional African rhythms with contemporary dance, creating a lively and engaging performance that draws in audiences. His success shows that by taking what already exists and adding your own twist, you can create something new and exciting.

So, you don't need to come up with a brand-new idea to make it shine in the market. You can take what's already there—just like Dangote and Diamond Platnumz—and transform it into something extraordinary with your creativity, making it truly memorable. This is how you discover a winning business idea and start your journey to something amazing. Let your dream, your big thing, come alive!

Key Stages for Creating Your Idea

Once you've decided to come up with an idea to start your own big thing, it's important to ensure that idea goes through the right stages to make it a reality. Think of creating a successful business idea like nurturing a newborn. Just as a baby grows through essential stages, a business idea also needs three key stages to develop and turn into a successful venture.

The first stage begins with identifying a problem that needs solving. Every successful business starts with a need, a gap in what's currently available, or a challenge people face each day. Reflect on the issues you notice around you. For example, you might realize that people in your neighborhood lack a place to buy freshly baked bread. Many rely on older options from grocery stores, with some lacking flavor because they have sat on the shelves for too long. Others have to search for better choices elsewhere, sometimes even traveling far to find quality bread. This absence creates a challenge, but it also offers you a wonderful opportunity to embrace.

Once you notice a problem, take some time to think about why it matters. Why does the absence of fresh bread impact people? How does it affect their daily lives? For instance, if there's no nearby source of fresh bread, people may buy lower-quality options that don't meet their standards or tastes. This can lead to dissatisfaction, especially for those who enjoy preparing meals with fresh ingredients. Write down the problem to help bring focus and direction, guiding you as you explore solutions. Make sure to describe the problem clearly while remembering that a successful business is always based on solving a real, meaningful issue.

The second stage involves identifying possible solutions. With a problem in mind, it's time to brainstorm ways to improve the situation. This stage calls for creativity and imagination. Ask yourself, "What can I do to make this better?" and let your ideas flow freely. For instance, one solution could be opening a bakery, a warm, inviting space where the air is filled with the aroma of fresh loaves, rolls, and pastries. You might offer varieties like whole grain or gluten-free options to cater to different tastes.

Another idea could be starting a bread subscription service, bringing fresh bread directly to people's homes. Think about the relief of busy families having quality bread delivered right to their doorstep! I'm sure this would save them time and effort, allowing them to focus on enjoying meals together. Alternatively, you could picture a small stand at a local market where you can offer samples, connect with customers, learn about their preferences, and build relationships. This personal touch can create a loyal customer base that appreciates not only the quality of your bread but also the care and attention you put into your business.

To develop your ideas, take a close look at each one through the lens of SWOT analysis: Strengths, Weaknesses, Opportunities, and Threats. Identify what makes each solution unique and how your resources or skills can give it an advantage, these are your strengths.

Consider any weaknesses and challenges you might face. Is there something you need to learn or improve? Recognizing these factors can help you prepare for what comes next. Look for opportunities around you, such as a growing interest in fresh, locally made products, and be aware of potential threats like competition or supply issues. Analyzing these elements helps you gain a clearer view of your ideas and the market. Remember, great solutions often come from careful thought and honest consideration.

The third and final stage is choosing the idea that is best suited for action. With multiple solutions in mind, it's time to select the one that aligns with both customer needs and practicality. Ask yourself if your chosen idea truly solves the problem you identified. If you decide to open a bakery, for instance, consider what types of bread your customers may want. Listening to their preferences helps ensure that your solution meets a real need in the community.

Profitability is another key consideration. Think about whether your idea will generate income. Ask questions like, "How much will it cost to start?" and "What should I charge for my bread to cover costs and earn a profit?" Developing a plan for how your business will succeed financially is essential to building a lasting venture. Look at the startup costs, ingredient expenses, and product pricing; all of these factors matter as you create a strong foundation for your business.

As you evaluate each option, consider the benefits and challenges of each. Your goal is to select a solution that inspires you and meets a genuine market need. Write down the strengths and any obstacles for each idea, helping you clearly see which option stands out.

Key Questions to Guide You

Now that you have built your business idea step by step, it's time to look at some important questions that will help you. Each question acts like a guide, helping you see what you truly want and how to get there. These questions are not just ordinary inquiries; they are keys that open the door to a better understanding of the journey ahead.

1. Does my idea solve a real problem? The heart of every successful business lies in providing a solution to something meaningful. A strong idea should help people, make their lives easier, or solve a challenge they face. If the problem is real, people will recognize the value in your solution and seek it out.

2. Is my idea realistic? While dreams are powerful, they need practical steps to become real. Focus on achievable goals today, knowing that you can expand and grow as you gain experience and resources.

3. What resources do I need to bring this idea to life? Resources like money, skills, technology, and connections are essential for bringing your idea to life. Understanding what you already have and what you need to seek through partnerships, training, or funding will be crucial as you move forward. You will explore this in more detail in Chapter 4.

4. Who are my customers? Your business needs customers to thrive. Understanding who will benefit from your offerings allows you to serve their needs better, helping your business grow stronger over time.

5. Is there enough demand for my idea? It's important to ensure there is enough demand for your idea. Researching the market can reveal real interest in your product or service. Even the best ideas require people's desire and support to become successful.

6. Can it make a profit? While passion drives you, profit keeps your business going. A good idea should generate enough income to cover costs and support growth over time, enabling you to reinvest and expand your reach.

7. What legal steps must I take? Every business journey has its legal requirements. Knowing the necessary permits, licenses, and regulations can keep you on track and help you avoid issues later on. You'll gain further insights on this topic in Chapters 5 to 7.

8. Who are my competitors, and what makes them successful? Learning from competitors who have traveled a similar path can provide valuable insights. Understanding what they do well can inspire you to create something unique and help you stand out in the market.

9. What challenges might I face? Every business journey comes with its own set of difficulties. Recognizing these challenges ahead of time can help you prepare and build confidence. By understanding potential obstacles, you can develop strategies to solve them, allowing you to navigate unexpected situations more effectively.

10. Does this idea align with who I am? Your business should reflect your identity and strengths. When your work aligns with your interests and skills, it brings fulfillment and motivation, even in challenging times.

11. How will I measure success? Success is more than just profit; it's about the impact you make. Setting clear goals helps you track your progress and keeps you motivated, reminding you of your original purpose.

12. Can my idea grow in the future? A lasting business can adapt and expand. Having the potential to reach more people or create new value ensures your journey remains dynamic and opens doors to new opportunities.

With these reflections, you'll gain greater understanding and confidence. You'll be prepared to build something lasting and meaningful, step by step, as your vision comes to life.

Business Ideas You Should Avoid

Coming up with the right business idea is an important step in becoming an entrepreneur. However, not every idea is a good one. Some may seem exciting at first, but they can cause big problems later. It's important to think carefully before starting any business. Therefore, any idea related to the issues we discuss here is not good for you at all, so it's best to avoid it to prevent future regrets.

Assume you're in a business where everything is always changing, and the rules keep shifting. This ongoing change can make it tough to predict what's coming next. This is what happens in unstable industries. When things feel unpredictable, it's hard to plan for the future. Before you start a business, ask yourself if the industry is safe and stable. If it feels like a wild ride, it might be better to look for something else. Think about how you would feel taking that risk. Would you feel comfortable dealing with constant changes? If that thought makes you nervous, it's a good sign to look for more stable options.

Let's say you're trying to open a bakery in a neighborhood where many people are struggling financially. If most of your neighbors can hardly afford bread, they likely can't afford to buy your fancy cakes and pastries. This means there might not be enough demand for what you want to sell. Before you choose what to offer, think about whether people in your community really need it. Ask yourself, "Will this be something they want or can afford?" If the answer is no, it's time to rethink your idea. Finding a product that meets the needs of your community can lead to success and bring joy to everyone.

It's great to be passionate about something, but that's not always enough to make a business work. You need to make sure people actually want to buy what you offer. Ask yourself if customers are interested in your products. If they aren't willing to pay for them, your passion alone won't help your business survive. For instance, you might love baking special cakes, but if no one wants to buy them, your business could struggle. To increase your chances of success, think about adding popular items that more people will want.

Some businesses depend too much on just one customer or a small group of people. If that one person decides to leave, your business could be in big trouble. Suppose you're starting a service only just for a friend. If that friend no longer needs your help, what happens to your business? You may find yourself with no customers at all. It's important to reach out to a wider audience so your business can grow.

Some ideas focus on short-term trends that might only be popular for a little while. When the trend fades, your business could disappear too. It's better to choose a business idea that can last. Think about selling items that everyone loved last summer. When that trend ended, many shops selling those items closed because customers stopped buying them. Ask yourself, "Will people still want this in a year or two?" If you're unsure, it might be better to look for something more timeless.

Don't ever start an illegal or unsafe business that could land you in jail. You might make some quick money, but it won't last, and the consequences can be serious. For example, trying to sell fake snacks or drinks. Not only is this illegal, but it can also harm people's health, leading to major legal trouble. Always think about the safety and legality of what you plan to sell. Would you feel proud to offer this to your community? If not, then stop it as soon as possible, and focus on something that you can stand behind.

By recognizing these potential problems, you can make smarter choices in your entrepreneurial journey. Avoiding business ideas that reflect these issues is crucial for building a successful business. Take the time to evaluate your ideas, ensuring they are safe and meet the needs of your target market. This careful thinking will help you build a strong foundation for your business and lead you to success.

Top Business Ideas You May Consider

Finding the right business idea can feel like a big challenge, and if you haven't found yours yet, don't worry, you're not alone. Many people struggle to come up with the perfect idea, but here's the good news: there are countless options just waiting for you.

Here are 135 exciting business ideas, each with potential in today's market. These ideas are practical and have proven to be successful. You can take one of these ideas and make it your own, allowing your dreams to shine through, whether you adjust it a little to fit your vision or completely transform it into something new. So, take a moment to explore them all.

1. *Accounting service*. This business idea involves managing finances for businesses by tracking income, expenses, and ensuring everything is correct.

2. *Adventure tourism company*. This business idea involves starting a company that organizes exciting outdoor activities, like hiking, rafting, or rock climbing.

3. *Affiliate marketing*. This business idea involves earning money by promoting other people's products and getting paid for every sale made through your recommendations.

4. *After-school program*. This business idea involves starting activities for kids after school hours to keep them engaged and learning.

5. *App development*. This business idea involves creating apps for smartphones or computers to help people with different tasks.

6. *Art classes and workshop*. This business idea involves teaching people how to paint, draw, or do other artistic activities.

7. *Art exhibitions*. This business idea involves creating a show where artists display their paintings, sculptures, or photographs for people to see.

8. *Art gallery*. This business idea involves establishing a place where people can see and buy artwork like paintings or sculptures.

9. Art supplies store. This business idea involves starting a shop that sells materials for making art, like paints, brushes, or sketchbooks.

10. Art therapy service. This business idea involves to use art to help people feel better emotionally and mentally.

11. Artificial intelligence consulting. This business idea involves helping businesses use smart technology to improve their services and make better decisions.

12. Automotive consulting. This business idea involves giving advice to car businesses on how to improve their services or sales.

13. Bakery. This business idea involves starting a shop that specializes in making bread, cakes, and pastries. The smell of fresh-baked goods fills the air, making it a sweet place to visit.

14. Banking, micro-finance & investment business. This business idea involves managing and growing money. It includes saving, lending, or investing in businesses to earn more in the future.

15. Bicycle repair shop. This business idea involves opening a store that fixes bicycles and sells bike parts.

16. Biodegradable product. This business idea involves creating items that break down naturally without harming the earth, like eco-friendly bags or packaging.

17. Biofuel production. This business idea involves making fuel from plants and other natural materials instead of oil.

18. Block chain solutions provider. This business idea involves offering services related to block chain technology, which helps keep digital transactions secure and transparent.

19. Business consulting. This business idea involves giving advice to companies on how to improve or grow their operations, sales, or products.

20. Butchery business. This business idea involves processing, selling or supplying quality meats to customers.

21. Car customization. This business idea involves modifying cars by adding special features, like custom paint, new interiors, or performance upgrades.

22. Car rental service. This business idea involves starting a business where people can rent cars for a short time, like for trips or events.

23. Car repair and maintenance. This business idea involves fixing cars when they break down or need routine services like oil changes.

24. Catering service. This business idea involves preparing and delivering food for events like weddings or parties.

25. Catering service. This business idea involves starting a service that prepares and serves food for events like weddings, parties, or corporate meetings.

26. Child enrichment program. This business idea involves starting classes and activities that help kids develop new skills like art, music, or science.

27. Childcare service. This business idea involves starting a service that cares for children while parents are at work. It provides a safe and fun environment for kids to play and learn.

28. Children's party planning. This business idea involves organizing fun and memorable birthday parties or events for kids.

29. Cloud computing service. This business idea involves offering online storage and computing power, allowing businesses to access their data and applications from anywhere.

30. Creative writing and publishing. This business idea involves writing and sharing stories, books, or articles with the world.

31. Creative writing workshops. This business idea involves establishing classes where people can improve their writing skills and develop their creativity.

32. Cryptocurrency trading. This business idea involves buying and selling digital money like bitcoin to make a profit.

33. Cultural exchange program. This business idea involves creating opportunities for people from different countries to learn about each other's cultures.

34. Cultural festival. This business idea involves creating large events that celebrate traditions, dances, and foods from different cultures.

35. Custom printing service. This business idea involves providing service that prints designs on items like t-shirts, mugs, or posters.

36. Customs brokerage service. This business idea involves acting as an intermediary between importers/exporters and government customs authorities, helping with paperwork and compliance.

37. Customs clearance service. This business idea involves managing the process of getting goods through customs, ensuring all documentation is accurate and compliant with regulations.

38. Cybersecurity service. This business idea involves protecting computers and networks from attacks and ensuring that sensitive information stays safe.

39. Daycare center. This business idea involves starting a place where parents leave their young children during the day while they work.

40. Delivery service. This business idea involves starting a business that delivers packages or food to people's homes or businesses.

41. Digital magazine subscriptions. This business idea involves owning online magazine of which people pay to read a magazine online instead of buying a paper copy.

42. Digital marketing agency. This business idea involves starting a company that helps businesses advertise online through social media, Search Engines Optimization (SEO), and other digital channels.

43. Digital product sales. This business idea involves selling things like e-books, software, or online courses.

44. Dog walking service. This business idea involves starting a service where someone walks your dog if you don't have time.

45. Drop shipping business. This business idea involves running an online store without holding any inventory, where products are shipped directly from suppliers to customers.

46. E-commerce store. This business idea involves creating an online shop where people can buy and sell products over the internet, making shopping convenient.

47. Electric vehicle charging. This business idea involves creating charging stations where electric cars can be powered up.

48. Electrical service. This business idea involves installing or fixing electrical systems in homes, like lights and power outlets.

49. Energy-efficient appliance sales. This business idea involves selling things like fridges, ovens, or light bulbs that use less energy and save money.

50. Environmental consulting. This business idea involves giving advice to companies or people about how to protect the environment.

51. Event planning and management. This business idea involves organizing events like weddings, concerts, or business meetings.

52. Exclusive content subscription. This business idea involves offering online content that is not available to the general public, for which people pay to access special videos, blogs, or tutorials.

53. Family counseling service. This business idea involves providing professional advice to help families solve problems and improve relationships.

54. Family health and wellness consulting. This business idea involves offering guidance to families on how to maintain good health, eat well, and exercise together.

55. Fashion boutique. This business idea involves starting a small, stylish shop that sells carefully selected clothing and accessories.

56. Film production company. This business idea involves starting a company that creates movies or short films.

57. Financial planning service. This business idea involves helping people or businesses organize their money and plan for the future.

58. Food processing and packaging. This business idea involves converting raw food into packaged products that are prepared for sale in stores.

59. Food truck. This business idea involves starting a mobile kitchen that serves delicious meals on the go. It parks at different locations, bringing tasty food to festivals, events, or busy streets.

60. Freelance writing and editing. This business idea involves writing or editing contents for websites, books, or businesses without being employed full-time.

61. Freight forwarding. This business idea involves managing the shipment of goods from one place to another on behalf of businesses, including coordination with carriers and customs.

62. Graphic design studio. This business idea involves starting a company that creates visual designs like logos, advertisements, etc.

63. Graphic novels and comic book creation. This business idea involves writing and drawing stories that are told with pictures and text, like comics or illustrated books.

64. Green building contractor. This business idea involves constructing houses and buildings that save energy and use eco-friendly materials.

65. Green energy solution. This business idea involves providing ways to harness energy from the sun, wind, or other natural sources to power homes and businesses.

66. Hair salon or barbershop. This business idea involves starting a place where people can get their hair cut, styled, or colored.

67. Home cleaning service. This business idea involves professionals who clean homes, leaving them tidy and fresh.

68. Home health care service. This business idea involves taking care of people who need medical help or assistance at home, like elderly or sick individuals.

69. Home renovation service. This business idea involves helping people upgrade or change parts of their homes to make them better or more modern.

70. Home security installation. This business idea involves helping people feel safer by installing alarms, cameras, and other security systems in their homes.

71. Homeopathic remedies. This business idea involves providing natural treatments that use small amounts of substances to help the body heal itself.

72. Human resources consulting. This business idea involves advising companies on how to manage employees, hire new staff, and improve the work environment.

73. Hvac installation and repair. This business idea involves installing and fixing systems that keep homes warm or cool, like air conditioners or heaters.

74. Hydroponics farming. This business idea involves growing plants in water instead of soil, usually in small spaces or indoors.

75. Interior design. This business idea involves helping people create beautiful and functional indoor spaces through expert advice and design.

76. Investment advisory service. This business idea involves helping people decide where to put their money to get the best returns.

77. Jewelry making. This business idea involves creating beautiful handmade jewelry pieces, including necklaces, bracelets, and earrings crafted from various materials.

78. Kids' activities and events. This business idea involves hosting or organizing events that entertain and educate children.

79. Land development. This business idea involves turning empty land into something useful like homes, businesses, or parks.

80. Landscaping design. This business idea involves designing beautiful outdoor spaces like gardens and yards for homes or businesses.

81. Laundry and ironing service. This business idea involves cleaning and ironing clothes for people who need help with these chores.

82. Leadership coaching. This business idea involves teaching people how to become better leaders and manage teams effectively.

83. Legal consulting: This business idea involves helping and advising people on legal matters in various areas.

84. Life coaching. This business idea involves guiding people on how to improve their lives, achieve goals, or feel happier.

85. Live streaming service. This business idea involves broadcasting live events or performances online for people to watch in real time.

86. Local delivery membership. This business idea involves offering a service where members pay to receive regular deliveries of food or other items.

87. Magazine publishing. This business idea involves publishing an internet-based magazine that covers topics like news, lifestyle, or entertainment.

88. Makeup artistry. This business idea involves starting a service that professionally applies makeup for events like weddings, parties, or photoshoots, helping clients look their best with expert techniques.

89. Marketing strategy consulting. This business idea involves providing companies with ideas on how to promote and sell their products or services.

90. Martial arts class. This business idea involves teaching self-defense and fighting techniques like karate, judo, or taekwondo.

91. Mental health counseling. This business idea involves providing support and therapy to help individuals cope with mental health challenges.

92. Mobile car wash and detailing. This business idea involves starting a service that comes to your home to clean and polish your car.

93. Music festival. This business idea involves creating big outdoor events where many musicians and bands perform.

94. Music production. This business idea involves creating, recording, and mixing music for artists or companies.

95. Nail salon. This business idea involves starting a beauty shop that specializes in manicures and pedicures. In this shop, people can relax while getting their nails painted and pampered.

96. Nutritional consulting. This business idea involves advising people on healthy eating habits to improve their overall health and well-being.

97. Online education platform. This business idea involves offering a wide range of courses on various topics online.

98. Online fitness coaching. This business idea involves providing fitness guidance and workout plans through the internet, making it easy for anyone to get fit at home.

99. Organic skincare product. This business idea involves producing or selling natural beauty products made without harmful chemicals, promoting healthy skin.

100. Organic waste collection. This business idea involves to collect food scraps and garden waste to turn into compost, which can be used in farming.

101. Organic waste composting service. This business idea involves to turn food scraps and other natural waste into compost that helps plants grow.

102. Painting and decorating. This business idea involves to make homes or buildings look new by painting walls and adding stylish touches.

103. Parenting workshop. This business idea involves to start classes that teach parents how to raise children well and deal with challenges.

104. Passenger transport service. This business idea involves to operate regular road, air or railway transport services to the people. This may be by airplane, helicopter, train or car.

105. Peer-to-peer lending platform. This business idea involves to own a website where people lend money to each other without going through a bank.

106. Performing arts school. This business idea involves to teach people how to act, sing, dance, or perform on stage.

107. Personal chef service. This business idea involves cooking meals for people in their homes, often tailored to their dietary needs.

108. Photography studio. This business idea involves establishing a studio where professional photos are taken, including weddings and portraits.

109. Plumbing service. This business idea involves fixing or installing water systems in homes, like sinks, toilets, or showers.

110. Property flipping. This business idea involves buying a home, renovating it, and then selling it for a higher price.

111. Radio station. This business idea involves broadcasting music or shows over the internet instead of traditional radio.

112. Real estate & property management. This business idea involves taking care of buildings, homes, or land. It includes buying, selling, and renting properties.

113. Real estate consulting. This business idea involves advising people on buying, selling, or investing in property.

114. Recycling and waste management. This business idea involves starting a service that helps people dispose of trash by reusing materials like plastic, paper, and glass.

115. Remote IT support. This business idea involves offering technological assistance to customers online, helping them solve problems without the need for in-person visits.

116. Renewable energy installation. This business idea involves setting up solar panels or wind turbines to use natural energy.

117. Roofing service. This business idea involves repairing or replacing the roofs of houses to protect them from weather.

118. Smart home installation service. This business idea involves setting up technology in homes that allows people to control lights, temperature, and security from their smartphones.

119. Specialty coffee shop. This business idea involves starting a shop that serves unique, high-quality coffee.

120. Specialty crop farming. This business idea involves growing specific, often unique crops like herbs, flowers, or rare vegetables.

121. Specialty food product. This business idea involves making unique or high-quality food items, such as gourmet snacks or organic treats.

122. Tax consulting. This business idea involves helping and advising people on tax matters.

123. Test preparation service. This business idea involves starting programs that help students prepare for important exams. These programs provide study materials and practice tests to boost confidence and performance.

124. Textile design. This business idea involves starting the art of creating patterns and designs for fabrics, such as clothes, curtains, or bed sheets.

125. Tour guide service. This business idea involves offering personalized guided tours to individuals or groups, showcasing local attractions, culture, and history.

126. Transport management software solution. This business idea involves developing software that helps businesses manage their transportation logistics, tracking shipments, and optimizing routes.

127. Travel agency. This business idea involves starting a company that helps people plan their trips. You find the best flights, hotels, and activities to make their vacation enjoyable and stress-free.

128. Travel blogging. This business idea involves writing and sharing experiences about travel online. As a blogger, you can provide tips, reviews, and inspiration for others planning trips.

129. Travel gear rental. This business idea involves starting a company that rents out equipment for your trips, like camping gear, bikes, or surfboards. It's a great way to travel light and still have what you need.

130. Upcycling business. This business idea involves taking old things and turning them into new, valuable items instead of throwing them away.

131. Urban farming. This business idea involves growing food like vegetables and herbs in cities, often in small spaces like rooftops or backyards.

132. Video editing service. This business idea involves taking raw video footage and editing it to create polished videos for personal or business use.

133. Videography service. This business idea involves filming events or creating videos for businesses, weddings, advertisements, or social media.

134. Warehousing and distribution. This business idea involves providing storage solutions and managing the distribution of goods to various locations, ensuring timely deliveries.

135. *Website design and development.* this business idea involves building and designing websites for businesses, blogs, or online shops.

Self-Reflection

Now, answer this exercise. It will help you in discovering a business idea that aligns with your path to success.

Questions	My Answer
1. What problem do I want to solve?	
2. How does this problem affect people's daily lives?	
3. What solution do I have in mind?	
4. What makes my solution unique?	
5. What are my passions and interests?	
6. Who is my target audience?	

7. What is my SWOT analysis?	
8. Is there a market demand for this idea?	
9. How will I handle competition?	
10. Is my idea long-term and able to grow?	

Figure 2.1: Self-Assessment Questions

Chapter 3

Writing Your Business Plan

"A goal without a plan is just a wish."

— Antoine de Saint-Exupéry

You've got your business idea, and that's a fantastic start! However, choosing the right idea alone doesn't guarantee success. You need a perfect business plan to bring your business to life.

In this chapter, you'll learn the benefits of a structured business plan and how to create one that sets you up for success. You'll gain insights on avoiding common planning mistakes and the importance of keeping your plan updated and staying committed to it.

By the end of this chapter, you'll not only have a clear, actionable business plan but also the ability to reflect on your progress, adjust where necessary, and confidently move forward with a solid foundation for success.

The Power of Your Business Plan

Back again in my MBA days, we had this unforgettable lecturer, Dr. Ikandilo Kushoka, who knew how to make us laugh while sharing serious wisdom. One day, he walked into class with a look that practically said, "Get ready; I'm about to drop some wisdom," and asked us, "What's your plan for studying this MBA?"

Now, you'd think a bunch of MBA students would have answers ready to go, right? Nope. We all froze, looking around like he'd just asked us to solve world hunger. Silence. Not a peep.

Dr. Kushoka smiled and said, "Alright, let me guess. Some of you are here because you're hoping your boss will notice your shiny new degree and say, 'Promotion time!' Some of you want that master's title so people will treat you like royalty. And a few of you just want to avoid disaster in your startup." We burst out laughing because he perfectly captured our thoughts!

Then he got serious, just for a moment, and said, "But here's the thing: each one of you had an idea to go to school and study, and you created a good plan to make it happen. You put that plan into action, and that's why you're here today." And that's when it hit me: without a plan, you're just wandering around, hoping for the best.

Starting a business without a plan? That's like trying to bake a cake by tossing flour, sugar, and eggs into a bowl and praying something tasty comes out. A business plan is a clear roadmap that tells you what you need to do and how to do it step by step, so you know where you're headed. It shows you what you want to achieve, who your customers are, and how you'll reach them.

And here's the cool part: a good business plan helps you see problems before they happen and find solutions early, making it easier to get through tough times. This is your chance to dream big and add some smart planning to keep everything on track. With a solid plan, you're not just throwing ingredients together and hoping for the best; you're baking a masterpiece that everyone will love!

Moreover, a business plan isn't just for you; it's also an important tool for sharing your ideas with others. Whether you're looking for investors, applying for loans, or just explaining your vision to friends and family, a clear and simple business plan helps others see what you want to achieve. It shows that you've thought through your ideas carefully and are serious about making your business a success.

Many businesses don't fail because the idea wasn't good. They fail because they didn't have a plan to make that idea work. Even if you have all the excitement and motivation in the world, without a plan, things can quickly fall apart. In other words, operating without a business plan is one of the main reasons most businesses fail to reach their potential. Having a clear plan is essential for staying on track and ensuring long-term success.

Now, take a moment and ask yourself: *Do I want to go on this business journey without a clear direction?* I'm sure you've heard stories of entrepreneurs who started strong but failed because they didn't have a solid plan. By understanding their mistakes, I believe you can avoid the same fate and not lose direction in your entrepreneurial journey. This is by taking the time to create a clear plan and set achievable goals that will guide you along the way.

Let me share the story of Mike Tyson, one of the most famous boxers in history. Throughout his boxing career, Tyson earned over $400 million. However, despite his success, he faced serious challenges after his time in the ring. In 2003, he declared bankruptcy in a U.S. court, stating he was $23 million in debt. This dramatic turn of events highlights the important role a solid business plan plays in achieving and maintaining success.

Tyson's downfall came from a lack of effective planning and financial management. He struggled with uncontrolled spending, made poor investment choices, and didn't have a clear approach to managing his wealth. His story serves as a powerful reminder that no matter how talented or famous someone may be, without a well-structured plan, the risk of failure remains.

Now, let's compare this with the success story of *Said Salim Bakhresa* from Tanzania, the founder of Bakhresa Group. His success serves as a powerful reminder of the importance of a solid business plan. Bakhresa didn't just have a dream; he took real steps, starting with a small restaurant named Azam in 1975. From the very beginning, he understood that success required more than just passion; it needed a clear plan.

As he looked to grow, Bakhresa expanded his business into various areas, including flour milling, beverages, and shipping. Each part of his journey was guided by a smart business plan that helped him understand the market, manage his finances, and tackle challenges with confidence. Today, Bakhresa Group stands as one of the largest companies in East Africa, showing what careful planning and hard work can achieve. His story is not just about building a successful business; it highlights how a solid business plan can turn dreams into reality.

Follow the path of *Said Salim Bakhresa* to succeed in your entrepreneurial journey. Don't be like entrepreneurs with great ideas and lots of passion but no clear plan, as you might end up like *Mike Tyson*. Remember, a business plan helps you see the way forward. Without it, you might find yourself going nowhere in the entrepreneurial world.

How to Write a Winning Plan

To write a winning business plan, imagine yourself guiding readers through a journey, a journey that reveals the dreams, strategies, and steps toward building something big. This plan isn't just a document; it's the foundation, and the inspiration for turning an idea into a thriving reality. Let's explore how to write each section of your business plan in a way that will capture your reader's attention, step-by-step.

The *Executive Summary* is the first section of your business plan. Think of it as a quick overview that explains what your business is about. Start with a brief description of your business, which includes a few sentences that say what you do. Next, write your mission statement, where you explain why your business exists and what change it aims to bring. After that, share a quick description of your product or service. You don't have to go into detail; just give a general idea of what you offer to make the reader want to know more. If you have any impressive financial highlights, like sales or growth numbers, now's the time to mention them to give a quick look into your success. End by painting a picture of your future goals, sharing your vision of where you're headed and how much you want to grow. Think of this part as the appetizer, offering a taste of what's to come and leaving the reader eager for the full story.

In the *Company Description*, you'll introduce the heart and soul of your business. Begin with the company history, sharing how your idea was born and how it developed into a real business. Think of it as your origin story, capturing the journey that brought you here. Then, share your mission, vision, and values. Your mission is the purpose of your business, your vision is where you want it to go, and your values are the beliefs that guide you. Write these in a simple way that shows what matters most to you. After this, write your business objectives. These are the main things you want to achieve, like increasing sales or expanding. Then, move on to your legal structure, describe whether you're a sole proprietorship, partnership, or limited company. Finally, talk about your location and facilities. Even if you're working from a small office or an online space, let the reader picture where your business lives.

Market Analysis is an overview of the world where your business will live. Start with an overview of your industry. Explain what's happening in this industry right now, like new trends or challenges, and how your business fits in. Then, describe your target market, or the people you want to sell to. These are your customers. Here, think as if you're talking to a friend: "Who are the people that would want to buy what I'm offering? What do they like?" The more details your friend provides, the easier it will be to define who you're selling to. The clearer you can see these people in your mind, the better you'll be at attracting the right customers for your business.

Then, take a step back to look at the overall market size and growth potential. This shows how big the opportunity is and why you're excited to be in this space. As you outline customer segmentation, break your audience into meaningful groups, identifying their unique characteristics and preferences. Finish up with a competitive analysis, where you take a friendly look at other businesses in your industry. Note what they do well and where you see a chance to stand out. This part is all about showing that you know your market and understand your place in it.

The *Organization and Management* section is all about showcasing the people behind your business. Start by describing your organizational structure, it's like introducing the team and showing how everyone fits together. List the leadership team and key roles, highlighting what makes each person a valuable asset to your company. Think of this section as presenting your team's talents and skills in a way that builds confidence in your reader. If you have a board of directors or advisors, include them here with a brief mention of their background and expertise. Then, outline the ownership structure, giving a clear understanding of who owns what share of the business. This section is about creating a sense of trust by letting readers know they're in good hands with your capable team.

When it comes to *Products or Services*, this is where you get to share your offerings with pride. Start with a description that brings your product or service to life. Think of this as if you're chatting with a friend at a gathering, sharing what makes your product special. Next, write about what makes your product different from others. This is your unique selling point and should show what makes your business special. After that, describe the product lifecycle, mapping out the journey from development to the hands of your customers. If you're working on new ideas or future versions, mention any research and development efforts here to keep the reader excited about what's to come. Wrap up with a look toward the future by sharing potential products or services that might emerge as your business grows. This section should feel simple and clear, helping readers understand what makes your business worth choosing.

Your *Marketing and Sales Strategy* is all about how you'll bring your product to your customers. Start by outlining your marketing plan, showing the different ways you'll connect with your audience, whether through social media, ads, or word-of-mouth. Think about how you'll spread the word and get people talking about your business. Then, write your sales strategy, describing how you'll make those connections translate into sales. Be clear and straightforward about your approach, whether it's in-store, online, or face-to-face. Pricing strategy is next, where you'll explain how you set fair prices that work for both you and your customers. Write down your plans for promoting and advertising your business, whether through ads, events, or other ways. Finally, write your distribution channels, showing the reader where and how customers can find and buy your product.

The *Operations Plan* is where you describe how your business runs day to day. Start by explaining the main steps in your operations. Write down the basic process of bringing your product to customers. Then, describe any technology or equipment you use, whether it's software, machines, or tools. Next, share how you keep quality high, showing that you make sure every product or service is good for customers. Describe your supply chain, explaining how you get materials or products and how they get to your business. Finally, include your inventory management if it's relevant, describing how you keep track of products. This section shows the reader that you've thought about the details of running your business smoothly.

In the *Financial Plan,* you'll share the numbers that support your business's future success. Begin with an outline of your revenue streams, showing where your income will come from. If you need funding, include your funding requirements, clearly saying how much you need and why. Next, show your profit and loss forecast, giving an overview of expected income and expenses. Keep it high-level, just enough to show your business is on a solid path. Don't forget to present a cash flow statement to show how you'll manage money day-to-day. Then, include a balance sheet, listing your assets and liabilities, to give a snapshot of your financial health. Finally, present your break-even analysis to show when you expect to start making a profit and cover costs. This section is all about confidence, showing readers that your business is built on a sound financial foundation.

If you're looking for investment, the *Funding Request* is your chance to share your needs and dreams. Start by explaining how much funding you need and be clear about the purpose of the funds. Describe how the funds will be used to grow your business, like hiring more staff, expanding marketing, or buying equipment. Mention any potential investors and stakeholders you're targeting, if you have them in mind. End with your financial projections if you get the funding, showing how the support will help your business grow. This section is about inspiring confidence and getting investors excited to join you on your journey.

The *Appendix* is a place for extra information. If you have resumes for key team members, add them here so readers can see their backgrounds. Include charts or graphs that explain your numbers or other details visually. If you have product photos, sketches, or samples, add them to help readers understand your product. If you have specific licenses or permits, list them here to show you're ready to operate legally. You can add any other relevant documents that support your plan. Think of this section as the bonus round, where you add anything that makes your plan even more convincing and complete.

Writing a business plan can feel like a big task, but with each section, you're building a strong foundation for your business. Approach it with excitement and pride, knowing that every section brings you one step closer to bringing your dream to life. With this guide, you're set to create a plan that feels genuine, inspiring, and ready to win over anyone who reads it.

Mistakes You Should Avoid

We all know that starting a journey without a map can lead to some wild adventures. You might find yourself in a strange place, wondering how you got there! Starting a business is similar. It's exciting, full of surprises, and sometimes a bit unpredictable. To truly enjoy the ride and find success, you need a solid business plan to guide you. As your *roadmap,* it helps you tackle any bumps in the road and make the most of the journey ahead!

Let's say you have a million-dollar idea, but without a plan, it's like bringing a rubber chicken to a cooking competition. Do you think you'll impress the judges? Probably not! You need a good plan that lays out your vision, sets clear goals, and outlines how to turn your dreams into reality. A good plan will not only keep you on track but will also help you celebrate each milestone along the way. When you have a plan, you can move forward with confidence, knowing you're one step closer to hitting the jackpot.

But hold on! Sometimes, big dreams can lead us to aim too high, pushing us into unrealistic territory. We might think starting a rocket company when we can barely launch a paper airplane! It's important to reach high but to keep our feet firmly on the ground. When creating your business plan, set goals that are within reach and realistic. This way, each goal you reach will feel satisfying and keep you encouraged, instead of weighed down by too much pressure. Setting realistic steps keeps you moving forward with energy and confidence.

Now, let's talk about the executive summary. Think of it as the movie trailer for your business, the first impression that grabs attention. If it's boring or confusing, no one will want to watch the full feature! A poor executive summary can make your business seem unpolished, missing a chance to show your best ideas. Take the time to craft a summary that hooks readers. Make it lively and clear, so they're eager to dive deeper into your plan. This is your moment to shine and show why your business could be the next big thing!

Length matters too. If your business plan feels like a big book, readers might lose interest! Just as people may feel overwhelmed by the sight of a lengthy book, they can be put off by a business plan that drags on without getting to the point. A big book can be hard to follow, and the longer it is, the more likely readers will skip important details or miss out on your key messages. To avoid this, keep your points clear and concise. A shorter, focused plan helps maintain the reader's attention and makes it easier for them to understand your vision. Your message should be like a catchy song, simple and easy to remember.

Supporting your ideas with facts is key. Assume you're telling a story about the giant fish you ate last week. If you can't prove it with a picture, people might think you're just spinning a tale! Readers want to see that you've done your homework. Use real data, examples, or anecdotes to back up your claims. This builds trust and shows that you're not just making things up as you go along.

Details are everything. Small mistakes can make you look unprofessional, like wearing socks with sandals! This silly fashion choice might make people laugh and show that you don't pay attention to details. n business plan writing, small errors, like typos, grammatical mistakes, and poor formatting are your enemies that can make readers doubt your abilities. Take the time to review your plan carefully to ensure everything is clear and neat. A polished plan shows you care about your business and makes you stand out to potential investors or partners.

Finally, remember that a business is all about the people. It's like a bus full of passengers, all eager to reach their destination. Now, suppose you're the bus driver but don't know how to drive! Instead of a smooth ride, you'll have chaos, wrong turns, and maybe even a few accidents. Now, think, would passengers be willing to get into a bus that could put their lives in danger?

Similarly, investors want to know who's at the wheel of your business and whether they can trust that person to guide the team safely to success.

Highlight your team's strengths and your role as a leader. Show that you not only have the skills to drive this bus but also the passion and dedication to ensure everyone arrives safely and happily at their destination. A great team can turn any idea into a successful business, steering it toward new opportunities and adventures.

By avoiding these common mistakes, you can create a business plan that makes readers smile and inspires confidence.

Update Your Plan

As you finish your business plan, remember this: your business plan isn't a dusty old book on a shelf; it's a living document that needs your care and attention! Think of it like your favorite playlist; sometimes, you need to change a few songs to keep the vibe fresh and fun. Why is updating your plan so important? Because the business world can be viewed as a roller coaster, full of unexpected twists and turns. To reach your long-term goals, you've got to stay flexible and go with the changes.

Let's look at Jack Ma, the mastermind behind Alibaba. He started with a simple idea: create an online marketplace for small businesses. Back in the late '90s, when the internet was just beginning to grow in China, many people were unsure about online shopping, just like they might be doubtful about pineapple on pizza. But Jack didn't give up! He and his team worked hard to connect Chinese manufacturers with international buyers, showing that shopping online could be safe and easy.

But here's where it gets interesting: Jack realized the world was changing faster than ever. With more people using their phones, he knew he had to update his business plan to make online shopping easier than ever. Instead of sticking to his original vision, he welcomed change and introduced mobile features and a user-friendly app that made shopping smooth and simple.

And it didn't stop there! Jack also noticed that customers wanted more than just a marketplace; they needed easy payment options and speedy delivery services. That's when Alipay came in, making online payments as simple as counting to three. He also invested in logistics to ensure that products reached customers faster than a cheetah on the move. This ability to adapt helped Alibaba grow into one of the largest e-commerce companies, valued at hundreds of billions of dollars.

Now think about a road trip. You begin with a clear plan, ready to start your journey. But then, you see a giant tree blocking your path, its branches spreading out as if it's trying to give you a big hug. Do you ignore it and keep driving straight ahead, or do you take a moment to find a new route? Successful entrepreneurs, like our friend Jack, choose to adapt. They pay attention to the signs and adjust their plans as needed because no one wants to find themselves stuck in a traffic jam!

Updating your business plan doesn't mean you've failed; it shows you're learning and growing. Each update is a golden opportunity to sharpen your vision and shape your goals. Think of it as sharpening a pencil. With each stroke, you create a finer point that allows for clearer and more beautiful drawings. Similarly, when you update your plan, you improve your strategies and become better prepared for whatever exciting adventures lie ahead!

Follow Your Plan

As you finish this chapter, take a moment to think about your business plan. Following it is important to keep your business on the right path. Your plan is a guide that directs your choices, keeps you focused, and helps you handle any challenges that come your way. By sticking to your plan, you make sure that your actions match your long-term goals.

Following your business plan takes discipline and commitment. It means doing what you've planned and making sure every choice supports your goals. Staying focused on your plan brings consistency, which helps your team and builds trust with your customers. Committing to the plan also helps you avoid distractions that can pull you away from what's important.

When things feel uncertain, your plan acts like a steady guide. By staying committed to it, you'll stay on track and move closer to achieving your goals. So, stick to your plan and enjoy the journey!

Self-Reflection

Now is the time to engage with the questions below to help you create a strong business plan that transforms your idea into action.

Questions	My Answer
1. How is my business plan like a roadmap to me?	
2. Why do I need a business plan for my new business?	
3. What are the key sections of my plan, and why does each matter?	
4. Have I done a SWOT analysis? What is one strength, weakness, opportunity, and threat?	
5. What signs tell me it's time to change my plan?	
6. What could happen if I start without a plan?	
7. What unique value does my business offer?	
8. How should I write my executive summary?	
9. Why should I see my plan as a living document?	
10. How committed am I to my plan?	

Figure 3.5: Self-Assessment Questions

Chapter 4

Resources and Location

"Success in business is not just about having the right resources; it's about having them in the right location."

— Donald Trump

You're holding your big idea, and your plan is set. It's like having a winning lottery ticket, just waiting to bring in the rewards! Now it's time to gather the right resources and pick the perfect location to start your dream business.

In this chapter, you'll discover how to gather and use business resources wisely, even if you're starting with limited funds. You'll also learn about choosing the right location, its costs and benefits, and options to set up your business in the best way.

By the end, you'll see how resources and location go hand in hand, how the internet can take your business anywhere, and self-reflection questions to ask yourself.

Business Resources

Let's take a look at a big town filled with talented people. The annual event "Town's Got Talent" was the highlight of the year. Local performers, including singers, dancers, and comedians, would showcase their skills, and everyone looked forward to the fun. This year, a young man named Hassan Mashaka was excited to perform his amazing juggling act because he is very skilled at throwing and catching several balls in the air at the same time.

As the talent show day approached, Hassan faced a big problem: he couldn't find his juggling balls! He searched everywhere but couldn't locate them. Feeling stressed, he sat on a bench in the park, worried about how he would perform. Just then, his neighbor, Mrs. Baraka, who loved crafting, walked by and noticed his worried expression.

"What's wrong, Hassan?" she asked, sitting down beside him.

"I can't find my juggling balls, and the show is tomorrow!" he replied, looking defeated.

"Don't worry! We can make new ones together," Mrs. Baraka said, her face brightening with a smile.

They headed to her house, where they found some soft fabric and stuffed it with old clothes to create new juggling balls. While they crafted, they shared stories and laughter, and Mrs. Baraka even taught Hassan some new juggling tricks. As they worked, Hassan realized he could use technology to improve his performance.

After they finished making the juggling balls, Hassan had an idea. He remembered seeing a tutorial on juggling tricks on YouTube. "I could record my routine and share it online! Maybe I can get feedback from others before the show," he suggested excitedly.

Mrs. Baraka helped him set up her tablet to film his practice. As he juggled, he noticed areas where he could improve. He shared his video with friends on social media like Facebook and TikTok, asking for tips and tricks. Their encouragement and advice gave him the confidence he needed.

On the day of the talent show, Hassan amazed everyone with his new juggling routine. He even incorporated some tricks he learned from Mrs. Baraka and the online tutorials. The audience cheered loudly, and Hassan ended up winning the top prize!

In today's world, business resources are like your best friends on the path to success. They include money, talented people, helpful technology, and useful knowledge. Just as Hassan relied on his neighbor Mrs. Baraka to help him create new juggling balls, every business needs these resources to thrive. Each resource, whether visible or not, helps shape the future of your business, giving you the power to be creative, adapt to changes, and succeed in a busy marketplace.

When we talk about business resources, there are several important types to consider. First, financial resources are like the fuel for your business. They include savings, loans, and investments that provide the necessary funds to start and grow. Just as Hassan needed materials to make his juggling balls, businesses need money to turn their ideas into reality and bring their visions to life.

Next, we have human resources, which focus on the skills and passion your team members bring. Like Hassan's experience with Mrs. Baraka, who provided guidance and support, your team is your greatest asset. Their hard work and dedication help move your business forward. Look at your team as superheroes, each with their own special abilities, ready to face challenges and celebrate wins together. Their collaboration can be the key to overcoming obstacles.

Then there are physical resources, the tangible things that keep your business running smoothly. These include equipment, tools, and the workspace where you operate. Just as Hassan crafted his new juggling balls, physical resources are essential for daily operations and ensuring everything runs well.

Intellectual resources represent the knowledge and ideas you and your team possess. This wisdom helps you make informed choices and stay ahead of the competition. It's like having a toolbox full of great ideas ready to use whenever you need them, similar to how Hassan used his juggling skills and learned new tricks to improve his performance.

Finally, we have technological resources, the software and tools that help you work better and faster. In today's digital age, these resources are important for connecting with others and getting things done efficiently. Just as Hassan utilized technology to record his routine and gather feedback, businesses can leverage technology to improve their productivity and make their operations run smoothly.

By recognizing and utilizing these essential resources, you can take your business to new heights! Just as Hassan found his star power through creativity and teamwork, you too can build a venture that not only achieves success but also brings joy to everyone involved.

How to Gather Your Resources

No matter whether you're starting a small business or planning a big project, understanding how to effectively gather your resources can help you obtain what you need for your dream venture. Think of it this way: your resources go beyond mere items; they are the essential tools that will guide you through the business world, offering the support you need to succeed. Each resource you gather is a stepping stone toward your vision, enabling you to face challenges, seize opportunities, and achieve your goals.

Financial resources are the lifeblood for your business operations. To gather these funds, consider beginning with personal savings, as this is often the easiest option. Talk to those around you and explore loans from banks or credit unions, which typically offer different financial products tailored for small businesses. Be sure to prepare a solid business plan that clearly outlines how you intend to use the funds and how you'll repay them; this can impress potential lenders.

And don't overlook the power of family and friends; they may be willing to invest in your vision. Crowdfunding platforms like Kickstarter or Indiegogo are also valuable avenues to gather funds from people who resonate with your idea. Reach out, share your passion, and let your excitement draw in support!

Let's move on to people resources, which include the skills, experience, and passion of your team. Building a strong team starts with clearly defining the roles and skills you need. Use job boards, social media, and professional networks like LinkedIn to attract potential candidates. Attend local networking events or industry conferences to connect with talented individuals who share your vision.

When hiring, look for a variety of skills and backgrounds; a mixed team can offer different ideas that encourage innovation. Once you have your team, invest in their growth through training and development opportunities. Regularly talk to them about their goals and aspirations, and make them feel appreciated. This will help you keep talent and improve their contributions.

Your physical resources form the foundation of your daily operations. To gather these resources effectively, create a detailed list of what you need, from office space and equipment to inventory. Research local suppliers and manufacturers for the best deals on equipment and materials, and don't be afraid to negotiate! Consider buying used or refurbished items to save money. For office space, look into shared office environments, which can provide a flexible and cost-effective solution. As your business grows, regularly reevaluate your physical needs and be ready to adjust to ensure you have the tools to bring your ideas to life.

Intellectual resources, such as the knowledge and insights you and your team possess, are valuable assets. You can develop these by committing to continuous learning: read industry-related books, attend workshops, and participate in online courses on platforms like Coursera or Udemy. Stay informed about market trends by following relevant blogs, podcasts, and news outlets. Encourage your team to share their knowledge and experiences, as creating a culture of learning within your organization can inspire creativity and innovation. Networking with mentors and industry experts can also provide insights that help you make informed decisions and stay ahead of the competition.

Lastly, consider the role of technology in your business. In this digital age, technology can revolutionize how you operate. To gather the right technological tools, assess your business needs and research software and applications that align with your goals. For project management, tools like Trello or Asana can help organize workflows. For financial management, software like QuickBooks or Tally simplifies accounting tasks. Explore communication platforms like Slack or Zoom to keep your team connected, regardless of their location. Many of these tools offer free trials, so take advantage of them to find what works best for you before committing to a purchase.

Remember that your resources are more than just tools; they play an important role in turning dreams into reality. By gathering and using the right mix of financial, human, physical, and technological resources, you build a strong foundation for a successful business. So, go ahead, reach out, engage, and gather the resources that will help you achieve your goals!

How to Use Resources Effectively

Using resources effectively isn't just a good practice; it's a game-changer for your business. With the right mindset to navigate your entrepreneurial journey, focusing on maximizing every dollar, skill, and tool, you will set yourself up for long-term success. This mindset is key to making informed decisions that drive growth and innovation, ensuring that each resource contributes meaningfully to your goals.

To begin, it's important to set clear, ambitious goals that guide how you use your resources. Look at your dream outcome, whether it's launching a new product or doubling your sales. By establishing clear goals, you turn tasks into purposeful actions, fueling motivation and giving direction to your team. These goals will serve as a compass, helping you determine where to focus your resources most effectively.

Next, recognize that your team is a powerhouse of potential. By encouraging teamwork and open communication, you can use their skills and insights to achieve greater results. Create team discussions where every idea is valued, leading to creative solutions that might not have been thought of before. Additionally, investing in training empowers your team, building their abilities and boosting their confidence. A well-equipped team is essential for maximizing the use of your resources.

Moreover, embrace technology as your partner. In today's digital age, using tools that improve operations and productivity is essential. Automation, for example, can free your team to focus on innovation, creating an efficient workflow where everyone is connected. By integrating the right technologies, you can improve processes, reduce waste, and enhance overall efficiency.

Staying flexible is also important; regularly reviewing how you use resources and being open to change can make a significant difference in your business. This mindset enables you to adapt to new opportunities and challenges as they arise. Encourage a culture of creativity within your organization, where obstacles are viewed as chances for innovation. When your team feels empowered to think outside the box, they are more likely to find unique solutions that contribute to your business goals.

By implementing these strategies, you'll make the most of your resources while inspiring growth and innovation. Remember that every resource is a tool; use them effectively, and watch your business thrive! With clear goals, a collaborative team, the right technology, and a flexible mindset, you can transform your approach to resource management and set the stage for long-term success.

How to Start with Limited Resources

Starting a business with limited resources may seem difficult, but it's absolutely possible with determination and the right strategies. Many famous entrepreneurs began their journeys with few resources and found ways to build their businesses into remarkable successes. The key is to be smart, creative, and willing to put in the hard work. Let me show you how some of the world's most successful entrepreneurs started from humble beginnings, and how you can follow in their footsteps.

Using your skills is a fantastic way to kick off your business. You don't need a lot of funds; what you truly need are the talents you already possess. Everyone has something they are good at, whether it's writing, designing, selling, or fixing things. The key is to tap into those abilities and use them as the foundation of your business.

Ralph Lauren, the founder of the world-famous fashion brand is a perfect example of how skills and passion can lead to a thriving business. He didn't start with millions in the bank. He began as a tie salesman, using his unique style and passion for design to create neckties that stood out. He didn't open a huge store right away; instead, he focused on a small, niche market.

Over time, his brand grew into the global empire it is today, known for its classic American style and iconic polo shirts. His story teaches us that by starting with the skills you already possess, you can build something bigger.

Using your skills means you're starting with something you already know and enjoy doing. You won't have to spend money learning new things or hiring experts. Whether it's designing, cooking, teaching, or something else, your abilities can be turned into a product or service that others will pay for.

Starting with What You Have (Bootstrapping) is another good strategy. The idea of bootstrapping means growing your business from the ground up, using only the resources you have on your own, whether it's time, money, or effort. Instead of looking for investors or loans, you rely on what you already have to grow step by step.

Larry Page and Sergey Brin, the founders of Google, are great examples of bootstrapping. When they started working on their search engine, they didn't have a lot of funds or big investors behind them. Instead, they made the most of what they had at their university, using computers, a small workspace, and their own knowledge. Rather than trying to build a huge company right away, they focused on creating the best product they could with the resources available. Their dedication and hard work eventually paid off, and Google grew into one of the most valuable companies in the world.

Bootstrapping forces you to think creatively and carefully manage your resources. It's about being frugal and making sure every dollar is used wisely. It allows you to maintain control over your business and avoid debt or giving away equity too soon.

Finding free or low-cost resources is easier today than ever before. With the internet, there are so many free resources available today to help you get started. Whether it's using free design software, learning new skills through YouTube, or marketing your business on social media, you can find what you need without spending a fortune.

Do Won Chang and Jin Sook Chang Do Won Chang and his wife Jin Sook Chang founded Forever 21, a popular clothing brand, with very limited resources. They made the most of free resources available to them, such as using social media and word-of-mouth marketing to attract customers. By leveraging these no-cost tools, they were able to build a fashion empire.

Free tools help you cut costs without sacrificing quality. You don't have to pay for expensive software or marketing when you can find equally effective options for free. This allows you to invest your money in other important areas of your business.

Starting small gives you a chance to learn and make mistakes without risking too much. Instead of trying to create a big business overnight, begin with a simple product or service, test the market, and build from there.

Ingvar Kamprad, the founder of IKEA, didn't start by opening a massive furniture store. He began his entrepreneurial journey by selling matches to his neighbors as a young boy. He slowly expanded his offerings, selling other small items like pens, picture frames, and household products. As he learned more about what people wanted, he began selling furniture, which eventually led to the creation of IKEA. Rather than rushing into the furniture business, he allowed it to grow naturally from his early experiences. Today, his company is one of the largest furniture retailers in the world.

By starting small, you lower the risks of failure. You can test your ideas and gather feedback before growing. This careful approach helps you build a solid foundation, ensuring that each stage is successful before advancing to the next one.

Looking for Alternative Funding Sources is a good strategy as well. If you need extra money to get started, there are other options beyond traditional bank loans. Crowdfunding, grants, and business competitions are great ways to raise funds without having to take on debt or give away control of your business.

Mukesh Ambani, the chairman of Reliance Industries, didn't rely solely on traditional loans to grow his business. Instead, he found creative ways to raise capital through partnerships and strategic investments. By thinking outside the box and looking for non-traditional funding sources, Ambani was able to expand Reliance into one of the largest companies in India.

Alternative funding sources like crowdfunding and grants provide opportunities to raise funds without having to pay it back or give up equity in your company. It's a smart way to find the resources you need without putting yourself under financial pressure.

Networking is a powerful tool that helps you grow your business by connecting with the right people. Building relationships with other entrepreneurs, mentors, and potential customers opens up opportunities you might not find on your own.

Roman Abramovich's story is a strong example of how networking can help you get ahead in business. He started with very limited funds, working various small jobs in Russia. But he made key connections during Russia's privatization period in the 1990s, which allowed him to acquire significant assets in industries like oil and steel. Through these relationships, Abramovich was able to build his wealth and gain control of major businesses, including the purchase of Chelsea FC. Today, he is one of the wealthiest individuals in Russia.

Networking opens doors. By meeting the right people, you can learn from their experiences, find new opportunities, and even secure partnerships that can help you grow your business. Sometimes, a single connection can lead to your next big thing.

Being creative and smart can help you start successfully. Challenges are inevitable when you're starting a business with limited funds. The key is to stay flexible, think outside the box, and come up with innovative solutions to problems that arise.

Bill Gates, the co-founder of Microsoft, faced many challenges in the early days of his company. There were moments when funding was tight, and competition was fierce. But Gates was creative in his approach to securing deals and improving his product. By staying focused on creating software that met customer needs and finding smart ways to grow the company, he was able to build Microsoft into one of the most valuable companies in the world.

When you're creative and adaptable, you can find ways to overcome financial limitations and other challenges. Instead of giving up when things get tough, you can think of new strategies and approaches that allow your business to continue moving forward.

Starting a business with limited resources is absolutely possible, as these examples show. The key is to use your skills, be resourceful, and think creatively. Start small, build steadily, and make connections with people who can help you along the way. Remember, it's not the amount of funds you start with that determines your success; it's how you use the resources, skills, and opportunities you have.

Business Location

Business Location Business location refers to the physical site where your business operates and conducts its activities. This can include retail stores, offices, factories, or warehouses. Choosing the right business location is crucial, just like picking the perfect stage for a performance. A poor stage makes it hard to attract an audience, leaving your show unnoticed. If your business is in a less desirable area, customers may struggle to find you or walk past without stopping.

On the other hand, a great location can draw people in and create excitement around what you offer. Whether you are opening a small shop, setting up an office, or starting an online business, selecting the right location is essential for your long-term success. A well-chosen site not only enhances visibility but also helps you connect with customers and build a thriving business.

Costs and Benefits of Your Location

When starting your business, choosing the right location is essential for your success. Your location serves as the foundation of your venture, shaping how customers view you and how easily they can find you. There are typically three primary types of locations to consider: urban areas, suburban neighborhoods, and rural settings. Each option presents its own unique costs and benefits, making it crucial to carefully evaluate which environment is the best fit for your business goals and needs.

Let's say you're opening your business in a busy city like Dar es Salaam. In such areas, you'll find many customers, which can lead to increased sales. Big cities are full of energy and opportunities for making connections with other businesses. However, there is also a lot of competition, which means you will need to work hard to stand out. Plus, rent and other costs are usually higher in the city, so you will need to manage your expenses carefully.

Suburban areas can be a good choice if you want a quieter setting. These areas often have lower rent than cities, which can save you money. With fewer businesses nearby, you may face less competition. However, there might not be as many people walking by your shop, so you will need to advertise more to attract customers. It's important to make sure that local residents know about your business, even if they don't pass by it every day. When residents know about your business and its offerings, they are more likely to recommend it to friends and family, ultimately driving traffic and sales.

Rural areas offer even lower costs for starting a business. You can find larger spaces at cheaper prices, which is great if you want to grow later. However, there are challenges, such as a smaller number of potential customers. Fewer people live in rural areas, which means you may need to think creatively about how to reach them. Getting supplies might also be harder, especially if the roads are not in good shape.

It's essential to think carefully about where to set up your business. Understanding the specific costs and benefits associated with each type of location will help you make an informed decision that aligns with your business model and target market. You should evaluate your unique situation, including your budget, customer demographics, and operational needs, to select a location that best supports your goals and contributes to your business's success.

Tips for Selecting the Right Location

Finding the right place for your business can feel like an exciting adventure, filled with the joy of seeing your ideas come to life. The best location is not only a physical space, but also a place that creates a welcoming environment to support your success and growth. Follow the tips we discuss here to help you find the perfect location for your business.

Let's start by considering how easily your customers can reach you. If your business is located in a place that welcomes everyone with open arms, where they can park their cars easily or hop on a bus without any hassle, it becomes much more convenient for them. If you're in a busy city like Dar es Salaam, try to find a spot near public transport routes or major roads. Can you think of a popular restaurant that everyone knows? That's the kind of visibility and accessibility you want for your business! You want it to be just as easy to find, making it the go-to place for your customers.

Next, consider the cost of renting or buying property. It's essential to find a balance between a fantastic location and a price that keeps your wallet happy. Renting a shop in a bustling area of Dar es Salaam will cost much more than in a smaller town like Morogoro. Before committing to a lease or purchase, look closely at your finances. Take a look at a scenario where you can run your business without the stress of bills piling up. It's all about making smart choices that allow you to enjoy your business while comfortably covering your monthly expenses.

Now, let's talk about visibility and customer flow. Your business should shine in a spot where everyone can see it and stop by. Assume you're in a lively area like Kariakoo Market in Dar es Salaam, filled with friendly faces and a lot of activity. Every passing person could be a potential customer, and each smile could lead to a new connection. The more engaging the surroundings, the more energy your business will attract.

Don't forget about the local rules and permissions. Every area has its own set of guidelines, much like a game with specific rules. In some parts of Tanzania, certain areas are designated for specific businesses, like factories or shops. You wouldn't want to set up a large manufacturing operation where it's not allowed, just as you wouldn't try to sneak into a concert without a ticket. Understanding these rules will help you set up your business in a way that feels right and keeps everything running smoothly.

Choosing the perfect location is an exciting step in your journey. With the right spot, you'll create a happy atmosphere where your business can bloom, and customers will feel thrilled to visit. So go ahead, dream big, and find that wonderful place where smiles and success await!

Options to Set Up Your Business

When you're ready to start a business, one of the first decisions you'll face is where to set it up. The location you choose can significantly impact your success. Different types of businesses perform better in different environments. Depending on the kind of business you want to run, you might need a retail shop, an office space, or a storage area for your products. Take some time to think about what will work best for your specific needs!

One option is starting your business right at home. This choice can help you save money, which is especially helpful when you're just beginning. Many small businesses, like online shops or those making crafts, often start in a home setting. However, consider how professional your business needs to be. Ask yourself: Is my home a good place to work? Also, think about any distractions that could make it hard to stay focused.

If your business needs customers to come in and buy things, then having a shop in a busy area is very important. Suppose your business is in a place on a busy street or inside a popular shopping mall, where people are constantly walking by. It will create a booming flow of potential customers. In short, being in a location with lots of foot traffic can bring many customers through your door. Don't forget to think about how easy it is for people to reach your shop. A good location can be the key to attracting more visitors and making it convenient for them to stop by.

For businesses that offer services or if you're working with a team, renting an office can be a great idea. Look for an office that's easy to get to, near important places like banks and restaurants. This not only makes it convenient for you and your employees, but it also helps clients feel welcomed when they visit. A friendly and professional office can leave a good impression on everyone who walks through the door.

If you make products or need a place to keep your stock, finding a warehouse or industrial space is important. These places are usually outside city centers, where there's more space and lower rent. A warehouse can give you room to store materials and products without feeling cramped. Just make sure the space has everything you need, like easy access for trucks and enough storage room for all your items.

Twin Tools for Your Success

Your resources and location must fit well together for your business to succeed. Even if you have the best resources, putting them in the wrong place could make things harder. For example, having great tools in a location that is hard to reach can cause delays and extra costs. On the other hand, choosing a busy location without enough resources to handle increased demand can overwhelm your operations.

Gathering the right resources and finding the ideal location are both essential in building the strong foundation your business needs. Think of them as the twin pillars holding up your dream. Without one, the other may falter. So, take the time to evaluate your resources, weigh your options for location, and ensure that they work together to set your business up for long-term success. Just like a tree needs strong roots and plenty of sunlight to grow, your business will thrive when it has the right resources in the right place.

Your Business, Anywhere

In today's interconnected world, where you set up your business doesn't have to hold you back. If you own a small shop in a rural area like Nyachilo Street in a village of Morogoro, Tanzania, selling beautiful handmade crafts, you might have once worried that your business would only attract local customers, limiting your growth potential. But thanks to the internet, that small shop in a village can now reach customers in big cities like Dar es Salaam, across Tanzania, and even faraway places around the globe.

The internet has transformed how people connect with products and businesses. Think about how companies like Amazon and Alibaba began, they started small, serving their local areas before expanding globally. These giants of commerce have shown us that the internet has the power to turn even the most local of businesses into international success stories. Today, it no longer matters if your shop is in a rural area, a village, or even a single room in your home. What matters is that your business is online, and once it's online, the whole world is your marketplace.

This digital shift means that geography is no longer a barrier to success. Whether you're running a craft shop in Morogoro, a food stand in a rural town, or a service-based business from a small office, the internet gives you the tools to reach new markets, expand your customer base, and grow your brand beyond borders. It's never been easier to create a website, join online marketplaces, or use social media platforms to promote and sell your products to a global audience. As long as you have access to the internet, the potential to grow is limitless.

Now, you may set your business at any location of your interest. With the technological resources enabled by the internet, you can connect to new customers, expand your reach, and market your products or services to people worldwide. The freedom to choose where you operate, combined with the power of technology, means your success is no longer tied to a physical location. With the internet as your gateway, the world is truly open for business.

Self-Reflection

Work through the questions listed in the table to strengthen your approach to the resources and location that align with your overall business goals.

Questions	My Answer
1. What resources support my goals?	
2. How will I find more human resources if needed?	
3. What skills guide my business choices?	
4. Where should my business be?	
5. Have you weighed the pros and cons of city versus suburban or rural settings?	
6. How will I handle location issues?	
7. Do my resources fit long-term goals?	
8. Am I ready to adjust my plans?	
9. How will I attract customers here?	
10. How can I use the internet to reach customers beyond my area?	

Figure 4.1: Self-Assessment Questions

Ticket 2

Your Legal Setup

Registering Your Business

"The entrepreneur always searches for change, responds to it, and exploits it as an opportunity. But first, they must establish a legal identity by registering their business."

— Peter Drucker

Some people think that having resources and a nice location is enough to launch their business. Sounds simple? You also need to register it.

In this chapter, you'll learn why registration matters and gain insights into your business structure, along with the registration steps involved for each. You'll also learn about annual returns and maintenance compliance, ensuring your business stays in good standing with the law.

By the end, you'll engage in self-reflection, make your business official, protect your name like a superhero, and check off all the necessary requirements.

Business Registration

Sometimes, you can think of business registration as giving your business its own birth certificate so everyone knows who it is! It's the fun process of officially recording your business with the government, making it a legal entity with its own unique identity. In Tanzania, you can register your business through the Business Registration and Licensing Authority (BRELA), where you get to pick a catchy name, choose a business structure, and complete the necessary paperwork. It's your business's way of saying, "I'm ready for bigger opportunities!"

Sharif Kassim, a determined young entrepreneur from Tanzania, had a vision. He wanted to make a difference in his community by starting a pharmacy business. With passion and commitment, he launched his pharmacy as a sole proprietor, offering essential medicines and health products. His dedication to customer service quickly set him apart, and word of his excellent service spread like wildfire. Customers traveled from near and far just to buy from him, and his clientele grew steadily.

But despite his success, Sharif encountered a major setback. He wasn't registered. Without this crucial step, he found himself unable to sign official contracts with suppliers or expand his services further. Many golden opportunities slipped through his fingers simply because his business lacked formal recognition.

In a dilemma, Sharif looked for advice and guidance. When he came to me, I explained the importance of proper registration and the doors it could open for his business. Step by step, I walked him through the process, and Sharif took immediate action. With determination, he registered his pharmacy business.

The change was incredible. Almost immediately, new opportunities started coming his way. Sharif secured his first major contract with a renowned pharmaceutical company, a milestone that transformed his business. From that moment on, the future seemed limitless.

Sharif's story shows that business registration is more than just a formality; it's the key to opening up many new opportunities. If you want your business to grow and succeed, completing this important step can make a huge difference.

Key Benefits of Business Registration

When you register your business, you are officially recognized as its owner. This means you have clear proof that you are the one in charge, protecting you from any disputes about who owns the business or its ideas. In Tanzania, registering with the BRELA ensures that no one else can use your business name. This is vital for protecting your brand, your hard work, and your reputation. Without registration, someone might use the same name, leading to confusion for your customers and jeopardizing your success.

Having a registered business also opens up more opportunities for financial support. Banks, investors, and government grants are more likely to pay attention to you when your business is legally recognized. Financial institutions prefer to offer loans and credit to businesses that have taken this important step. Once you register, you can open a business bank account, which allows you to access special financial services designed just for businesses. This can be a game-changer when your business begins to grow and you need extra funds to keep moving forward.

Another benefit of registering your business is that it allows you to file taxes as a legal entity. Some people might see this as a burden, but it can actually provide you with advantages. By filing taxes, you can tap into government programs, receive tax breaks, and gain support for small businesses. Moreover, being compliant with tax laws means you avoid costly fines and penalties that can come from operating without registration.

In the world of business, conflicts can arise. You may find yourself in disagreements with customers, suppliers, or competitors. If your business isn't registered, any legal actions against you could affect you personally, putting your belongings and income at risk. However, when your business is registered, it stands as its own legal entity. This separation protects your personal property from business debts, especially if you run a Limited Liability Company (LLC). This means your responsibility is limited to what your business owns, giving you peace of mind.

Registering your business also opens doors to exciting partnerships and growth opportunities. Larger companies, government agencies, and international clients prefer to work with registered businesses because they provide trust and legal protection. If you have dreams of expanding beyond your local market, having a registered business is essential.

In today's global marketplace, many businesses aim to reach customers beyond their home country. However, without registration, this goal becomes difficult. When you register your business, you can participate in international trade agreements, obtain export licenses, and protect your brand in foreign markets.

Overall, registering your business is a smart decision that helps you build a strong foundation for future success. It opens the door to many benefits that can help you grow, thrive, and achieve your dreams.

Types of Business Structures

When you start the exciting journey of starting your business, one of the most important choices you'll make is selecting the right structure for it. This decision shapes how your business operates, how you handle taxes, how you raise funds, and how you protect your personal belongings. Let's dive into the types of business structures that can help you find the best fit for your needs.

If you're looking for the simplest way to start a business, a *sole proprietorship*, often called *a "solo business,"* is the way to go. In this setup, one person owns and runs the business, meaning there's no legal separation between you and your business. As the "solo" owner, you make all the decisions, control operations, and keep all the profits. Sounds great, right? But here's the catch: you also take on all the risks by yourself. If the business runs into debts or legal issues, your personal assets could be on the line. It's like being the captain of a ship. You're in charge, but you also have to face any challenges that come your way.

Now, if you're not ready to take on everything alone, a *partnership* might be a better choice. This is when two or more people team up to run a business. A partnership allows you to share responsibilities, resources, and ideas with others. Each partner brings their own skills, money, or resources to the table, and you share the profits, risks, and losses. While this setup can lighten your load, remember that everyone involved is still financially liable for the business's obligations. It's like a group of friends sharing a pizza, everyone gets a slice, but you all chip in for the bill!

For those seeking a more formal approach, a *company* is a great option. This structure legally separates the business from its owners, known as shareholders, which means you're not personally responsible for the company's debts. Companies come in several types, each with its unique flavor.

Some types of companies include a *private company,* which is owned by a small group, such as family members or investors, and doesn't sell shares to the public. On the other hand, a *public company* offers shares to anyone who wants to buy them on the stock market, but it must follow strict rules and share its financial information with the public. Lastly, a *foreign company* is established in one country but operates in multiple countries, giving it a global reach. This allows it to spread its wings and tap into new markets around the world!

How to Register Your Business

Every entrepreneur looking to start a business must understand the steps involved in the registration process to ensure everything goes smoothly. Whether you're setting up a sole proprietorship, partnership, or company, each business structure comes with its own set of rules, and understanding these is crucial for a successful registration. Now, let's go through the process of how to register them:

1. Pick a name for your business. The name should be unique, catchy, and clearly reflect what you do. If you're registering a sole proprietorship or partnership, avoid using just a personal name like "Patricia." Instead, go for something like "Patricia Traders" or "Patricia Company" so it's clear that you're running a business, not just using a personal name. Your business name should include terms like "business," "enterprise," "company," "investment," "suppliers," "traders," or something relevant to your activity.

For companies, ensure that the name ends with "Limited." Be original, and avoid copying names of registered businesses, as this could lead to rejection. You can check if your chosen name is available by visiting BRELA's online platform *(https://ors.brela.go.tz)* and using their name search tool, as explained in step 4.

2. Draft a constitution for your business. If you're a sole proprietor, skip this step. For partnerships, it's optional, but it's highly recommended to have a partnership agreement. This document outlines each partner's role, responsibilities, and profit-sharing terms, helping you avoid conflicts in the future.

For companies, a constitution is required and typically consists of the "Memorandum and Articles of Association." The Memorandum covers the company's name, office, purpose, and shareholder details, while the Articles outline the rules of operation, including the roles of directors and shareholders. Together, these make up the legal foundation for your company.

3. Access the BRELA Online Registration System (ORS). Go to the ORS website *(https://ors.brela.go.tz)* to access your account. If you don't already have an account, you'll need to create one. For Tanzanians, select "Create ORS Account" and fill in the following details:

- Captcha information.
- Date of birth.
- Email address.

- Mobile phone number.
- National ID number.
- Nationality.
- Password (insert the same password twice).

For foreigners, choose "Create ORS Account" as well and fill in the following details:

- Captcha information.
- Country of passport issuance.
- Date of birth.
- Email address.
- Middle and last name.
- Mobile phone number.
- Nationality.
- Passport number.
- Password (insert the same password twice).
- Your gender options.

Once you're done, tick the checkbox to agree to the terms and submit your account creation. You'll receive a username by email, which you can use to log in and manage your registration. If you already have an ORS account, select "E-Services for Registered Users," enter your username and password, and sign in.

4. Fill the Online Application Form. After signing in to your account, you'll arrive at the registration screen, which has two main buttons: "New E-Service" (used for registering your business name) and "Name Clearance" (used to check if your chosen name is already in use or similar to another). Click "Name Clearance," type your preferred name in the search field, and review the results to see if any names are too similar. Avoid names that show a similarity of more than 10 to 15 percent, as this may lead to rejection or delays. After confirming your name is unique enough, you can start your registration process.

All sole proprietorship and partnership names are registered under the "Business Name" option. If your business falls under one of these structures, select "New E-Service" and choose "Business Name." Click "Proceed" after each step. Then, select "Registration of New Business Name." Next, choose the ownership type of the business name: "Individual (sole proprietor)," "Partners," or "Corporation" (if an already registered company wants to own a business name). Then, fill in the following details:

- Contact details (for you or each partner).
- Full name (for you or each partner).
- National identification or passport number (for you or each partner).
- Postal address (if you don't have a P.O. Box yet, you can use a close person's address for temporary).
- Proposed business name, activities, and address.
- Residence address (for you or each partner).

After filling in the required details as shown above, click "Proceed" and refresh to generate a consolidated application form. Print this form, sign it, and add a company stamp anywhere within the form if the business name is owned by a registered company. After signing, scan the document and proceed to the next step.

For a company registration, select "New E-Service" and choose "Company." Complete the registration by selecting the company type. If you're registering a local business, select either a private or public company limited by shares. If you're registering a foreign company, there's an option to use your original foreign company's name.

For a private or public company limited by shares, fill in the following necessary details:

- Amount of share capital authorized.
- Classes of authorized share capital.
- Company accounting date.
- Company activities.
- Company contact details.
- Company office address.
- Company secretary with his/her ID number, contact details, and residential address.

- List of Directors with their ID numbers, contact details, residential addresses and Tax Identification Numbers (for Tanzanians).
- List of shareholders with their numbers of share ownership, ID numbers, contact details, and residential addresses.
- Persons who can update data in ORS.
- Postal address (if you don't have a P.O. Box yet, you can use a close person's address for temporary).
- Proposed company name.

For a foreign company, fill in the necessary details listed below:

- Charges.
- Company accounting date.
- Company activities.
- Company contact details.
- Company office address.
- Company secretary with his/her ID number, contacts, and residential address.
- Date of incorporation in the country of origin.
- Incorporation number in the country of origin.
- List of Directors with their ID number, contacts, residential addresses and Tax Identification Number (for Tanzanian).
- List of persons entitled to charge.
- Persons resident in Tanzania authorized to accept service on behalf of the company with their ID number, contacts, residential addresses and Tax Identification Number (for Tanzanian).
- Persons who can update data in ORS.
- Postal address (if you don't have a P.O. Box yet, you can use a close person's address).
- Proposed company name.
- Registered office address in the country of origin.

After filling in all the required details for either a private and public company limited by shares or a foreign company, click "Proceed" and refresh to generate two forms: the consolidated application form and the ethics and integrity form. Print both forms. Then, sign the printed forms. Ensure that the ethics and integrity form is signed only by the CEO of the company and stamped with the company stamp. After that, scan the signed documents along with any other necessary additional documents, and get ready to move to the next step.

5. *Upload the Required Documents.* If you logged out, log back into your account and navigate to the "My List" section on the left-hand side to find your incomplete application and click it. Then, you will need to upload the required documents based on your business structure, as instructed here.

For your sole proprietorship or partnership business, upload the following documents:

- A copy of identification documents for all foreigners (for you or each partner).
- Partnership agreement if available).
- The scanned application form you printed and signed.

For your private or public company, attach:

- A memorandum and article of association.
- Declaration of Compliance on Application for the Registration of a Company (form no. 14b).
- The identification documents (only for foreigners).
- The scanned consolidated application form you printed and signed.
- The scanned ethics and integrity form you printed and signed.

For your foreign company, upload:

- Certificate of Incorporation (from the Parent Country).
- Incorporation document.
- Most recent audited accounts.
- Return and declaration delivered for registration by a Foreign Company (form n. 434).

- The identification documents (only for foreigners).
- The scanned consolidated application form you printed and signed.

Make sure you carefully review all the information you provided to ensure its accuracy. Once you're satisfied that everything is correct, click the "Submit" button to send your application for processing.

6. *Pay Registration Fees.* After submitting your application, you will be prompted to pay the registration fee, based on the details below:

Details	Total Fee
For individual (sole proprietorship) or partnership business	TZS 20,000
Foreign company (share capital size is not applicable)	USD 1,190
For company with share capital of more than TZS 20,000/= but not more than TZS 1,000,000/=	TZS 167,200
For company with share capital of more than TZS 1,000,00[0/= but not more than TZS 5,000,000/=	TZS 247,200
For company with share capital of more than TZS 5,000,000/= but not more than TZS 20,000,000/=	TZS 332,200
For company with share capital of more than TZS 20,000,000/= but not more than TZS 50,000,000/=	TZS 362,200
For company with share capital above TZS 50,000,000/=	TZS 512,200

Figure 6.1: Registration Fees

The fees can be paid via various methods listed on the BRELA platform, including bank transfer or mobile money. After payment, you should receive a confirmation email indicating that your payment was successful and that BRELA is processing your application.

7. Waiting for Your Application Approval. After submitting your application, BRELA processes it in three stages, each taking around three days. The first stage is called "Process and Enter Recommendation," where BRELA reviews your application to ensure there are no errors, particularly in completing the online forms and attaching all necessary documents.

If there are any issues or missing documents, your application will be rejected. In such cases, you can navigate to the "My List" section, find your rejected application, and click to edit it. After making the necessary corrections, click "Proceed," then refresh to generate the forms again. Once done, sign, scan, upload, and submit the updated documents.

The second stage is called "Final Decision," where BRELA confirms that your application is correct and begins finalizing your registration. The final stage is "Registered," during which BRELA approves your application, generates your registration documents, and sends them to you. You will receive an email notification once your application has been successfully registered.

8. Obtain Your Registration Documents. To obtain your official registration documents, log back into your ORS account and go to the "My Application" section. Locate your application and download the registration documents.

For sole proprietorship or partnership businesses, you will receive two documents: the *Certificate of Registration,* which proves that your business is officially recognized in Tanzania, and the *Extract from the Registrar,* which contains details about your business, such as its registration status and activities.

For companies, you will receive either a *Certificate of Compliance,* which confirms that your foreign company is officially recognized in Tanzania, or a *Certificate of Incorporation,* which confirms that your local company is officially recognized in Tanzania.

Annual Return

In Tanzania, every registered company is required by law to submit an annual return to the BRELA, as per the Companies Act of 2002. This isn't just a formality, it's a legal obligation. Failing to submit on time could result in a fine of TZS 2,500 for every month of delay. That penalty can quickly add up, so it's best to stay on top of it and keep your business on track.

To keep everything running smoothly, make sure to submit your annual return within 28 days of your company's formation date each year. This isn't just another boring piece of paperwork; it's a summary of your company's activities over the past year. Think of it as a yearly report card that lets you track your growth and see how far you've come.

Filing your annual return on time is super important for keeping your business in good standing. If you miss the deadline, you risk putting your company's legal status in jeopardy, which can affect your ability to operate, secure loans, or even attract new customers. So, treat submitting your annual return like a crucial part of being a responsible entrepreneur in Tanzania. By staying on top of your obligations, you're not just protecting your business; you're paving the way for future success. So, grab a calendar and make this task a top priority!

Annual Maintenance Fee

If you're operating a registered business name in Tanzania, there's an essential fee you need to be aware of: the annual maintenance fee. Set at just TZS 5,000, this fee is due every year to the BRELA. It applies to all business names registered under the Business (Registration) Act of the United Republic of Tanzania, regardless of whether the business is owned by an individual (sole proprietor), a partnership, or a registered company. It's important to note that business names and company names are governed by different laws, so don't confuse the two.

Now, you might wonder why this fee matters. Paying the annual maintenance fee keeps your business registration up to date and helps cover the costs of managing official business records. As an entrepreneur, being aware of this fee and paying it on time shows your commitment to following the legal requirements of running a business. It protects your business name and helps keep your operations running smoothly.

Self-Reflection

Reflect on the self-questions below to assess your understanding of this chapter before moving on to the next page.

Questions	My Answer
1. Why should I register my business?	
2. What could I miss out on if I don't register?	
3. How would registering help me?	
4. What structure fits my business idea?	
5. Does my business name reflect my brand?	
6. Do I know how to register locally?	
7. How could registration benefit me financially?	
8. Am I aware of the annual fees and returns?	
9. What worries do I have about registration?	
10. What steps will I take to register?	

Figure 6.2: Self-Assessment Questions

Chapter 6

Obtaining Tax Documents

"In the business world, the rearview mirror is always clearer than the windshield. You need accurate tax documents to navigate forward successfully."

— Warren Buffett

You've successfully registered your brand name, and that is a big milestone! Now, you're ready to take the next step: getting your business recognized by the Tax Authority. This step not only prepares you to obtain tax documents but also run your business without any tax issues down the road.

In this chapter, you'll uncover the various tax documents you need and how to obtain them. We'll discuss how much you need to pay and explore other essential tax compliance matters that are important for your business.

By the end, you'll assess on your understanding and feel empowered to take charge of your journey.

Pay Your Taxes

Taxes are often a source of fear for many entrepreneurs. While they may not be the most exciting aspect of running a business, they are essential for sustainable growth. Every entrepreneur should know who to contact for assistance with tax matters. In mainland Tanzania, the Tanzania Revenue Authority (TRA) oversees all tax-related issues. If you are in another country, remember that each has its own tax authority responsible for similar functions.

In recent years, tax authorities have made it easier for entrepreneurs by digitizing their services. No longer do you have to stand in long lines at a tax office; now, most documents can be obtained online. In Tanzania, for example, the TRA introduced an *e-filing system,* allowing you to register, file taxes, and obtain certificates from the comfort of your home. Similar systems are now available in many places around the world.

Paying your taxes is not just a legal obligation; it's also important for your business and the country as a whole. Let's break it down: taxes are the fuel that keeps a nation running. They help build roads, schools, and hospitals, and they support the infrastructure that allows businesses like yours to grow.

You've probably heard stories of businesses forced to close because they didn't comply with tax laws and pay their taxes. Let me tell you about my client, Seif Pempas, an enthusiastic entrepreneur from Kariakoo with big dreams of making money by selling diapers in Tanzania. He started importing a brand called Predo diapers from Turkey, confident he would be swimming in profits in no time.

One day, he came to me with a request: "I want to pay less tax. How can I keep more of my money and pay as little as possible?" He was already dreaming of counting his profits, but I gave him my honest advice. I explained that following Tanzania's tax laws would save him trouble in the long run. I even told him about the potential benefits, like government contracts, loans, and other opportunities that come with being tax-compliant.

But Seif wasn't convinced. He smiled confidently and said, "Why should I give all my hard-earned money to the taxman? I'll keep my cash right here, thanks!" With that, he went off, determined to avoid as many taxes as he could.

For a while, everything seemed fine. Seif's business was running, diapers were selling, and he was happy. But soon enough, TRA took notice. They hit him with a mountain of fines and penalties so high that he could hardly see over them! His dream business was buried in debt, and there was no way he could pay it all off. With a heavy heart, Seif had to shut down his company.

Years later, Seif returned to me, looking a bit more experienced. He laughed sadly and said, "I should have listened to you! My company could have been the biggest diaper supplier in Tanzania by now." He was full of regret but also eager to fix his mistakes.

Luckily, there was a way forward. With the help of TRA, we worked out a plan for him to pay his tax debt in small installments. Seif's business slowly came back to life. Now, he's working every day, paying off his debts, and keeping his company going. He's learned that paying taxes isn't just about avoiding fines; it's also a way to support his country and create a better future for everyone.

Today, Seif laughs at his own story, sharing it with other entrepreneurs as a lesson. "Don't be like me!" he says with a smile. "Pay your taxes, follow the rules, and save yourself the headache." His journey taught him that sometimes, the long road is the best road to success. o, as an entrepreneur, make sure you comply with tax laws and clear your tax debts to avoid any consequences later on.

Tax Certificates

Tax certificates are not just administrative requirements; they are essential documents for running a legal and successful business. Securing the right tax certificates ensures that your business is compliant with government regulations and positioned to succeed in competitive markets. These certificates open up new opportunities for contracts, government tenders, loans, and other business opportunities that can help your business grow. They include: identification number certificate, tax clearance certificate, withholding tax certificate, value added tax registration certificate, excise duty registration certificate, capital gain tax certificate.

TIN Certificate

A Tax Identification Number (TIN) is a unique number given to every person registered with the tax authority. This number helps the government track and manage tax obligations for both individuals and businesses. After registration, a TIN certificate is issued to show that the person is recognized by the tax authority as a taxpayer.

Getting a TIN certificate is often the first step in setting up your business in the tax system. Without it, your business is considered informal and may face legal issues, fines, or penalties. The TIN certificate is essential for many activities, such as opening a business bank account, filing tax returns, applying for business licenses, and seeking government contracts or tenders.

In Tanzania, the documents needed to get a TIN depend on the structure of your business. The requirements vary for a sole proprietorship, a partnership, or a registered company. Understanding these differences will help you prepare and make the application process smoother.

If you are a sole proprietor, you will need to submit:
- An introduction letter from the local government where the business is located.
- Certificate of registration and extract from the registrar (this is applicable only if registered with BRELA).
- Lease agreement.
- National ID, driving license, voter ID, or passport.
- One passport-size photo.

For a partnership, the following documents are required:

- An introduction letter from the local government where the business is located.
- Business name registration certificates of your partnership (certificate of registration and extract from the registrar).
- Lease agreement.
- National ID, driving license, voter ID, or passport of each partner.
- Partnership deed (optional).
- Two passport-size photos of each partner.

If you're applying for a TIN for a registered company, you will generally need:

- An introduction letter from the local government where the business is located.
- Certificate of incorporation.
- Lease agreement.
- Memorandum and Articles of Association.
- National ID, driving license, voter ID, or passport of each director or owner.
- Two passport-size photos of each director or owner.

The process for obtaining a TIN certificate depends on the business structure. For sole proprietors, it's usually simpler with fewer documents. In partnerships or registered companies, it involves more detailed documentation due to multiple partners or directors.

TC Certificate

A Tax Clearance Certificate (TCC) is a document from the tax authority that confirms a business has met all tax obligations. It shows that there are no outstanding taxes, unpaid penalties, or compliance issues, indicating good standing with the tax authority. This certificate is often required when:

- Applying for government contracts or tenders.
- Applying for business licenses.

- Seeking investments or partnerships.

Many entrepreneurs overlook the importance of a TCC until they miss out on big opportunities. Having this certificate ready means you can pursue new ventures without delays due to tax issues. No matter your business type, you will need the following to apply for a TCC:

- An application letter for the tax clearance certificate.
- Proof of payment showing all due taxes are paid.

Withholding Tax Certificate

A Withholding Tax Certificate is issued to confirm that a business has correctly paid withholding tax. This tax is important in transactions with contractors or suppliers for services, as it involves deducting a portion of their payment as an advance income tax. Withholding tax applies to various payments, such as dividends, professional services, rental income, and other contracts.

By deducting withholding tax, you fulfill a legal requirement and assist contractors in managing their tax payments. The withheld amount eases their tax burden when they file annual returns, making financial planning simpler. Below are common withholding tax rates for various transactions:

Withholding Tax on	For Resident	For Non-Resident
Dividends (non-listed companies on DSE)	10%	10%
Dividends (listed companies on DSE)	5%	5%
Rents for land and buildings	10%	20%
Rents for construction equipment/machinery	10%	10%
Professional and other service fees	5%	15%
Non-full-time director fees	15%	15%
Interest payments	10%	10%

Commission on mobile money transfers	10%	N/A
Bank commissions and digital service agent fees	10%	N/A
Management/technical fees (mining, oil & gas)	5%	N/A
Royalties	15%	15%
Film industry royalties	10%	10%

Figure 7.3: Withholding Tax Rates

VAT Certificate

Value-Added Tax (VAT) is a tax applied to the sale of goods and services, and it's a significant revenue source for the government, ultimately borne by consumers. In Tanzania, if your business meets VAT registration requirements, it becomes mandatory to register. Upon successful registration, you will receive a VAT certificate, allowing you to collect VAT from customers and remit it to the government. Many businesses, particularly those dealing with large corporations, government entities, or international clients, prefer to work with VAT-registered businesses.

In Tanzania, businesses with an annual turnover exceeding TZS 200 million are required to register for VAT. This threshold may change based on decisions by the TRA or Ministry of Finance to adapt to economic conditions. However, registration may also be necessary even if your turnover is below this threshold, depending on the nature of your business activities. For example, if you provide specific taxable services or sell products that are subject to VAT, you may still need to register. This applies particularly to businesses in sectors like telecommunications, hotel services, and other industries identified by the TRA as requiring

VAT registration. Additionally, if you engage in economic activities involving the supply of professional services in Mainland Tanzania or are an intending trader, registration becomes mandatory.

Once registered, your business must charge VAT on sales. The standard VAT rate in Tanzania is 18%. This means you add 18% to the selling price of goods or services. For example, if you sell a product for TZS 1,000, you will charge TZS 1,180, with TZS 180 being the VAT amount.

VAT-registered businesses can reclaim VAT paid on business-related purchases, called input tax. This process ensures businesses aren't taxed multiple times on the same goods and services, as VAT is ultimately meant for the final consumer. For instance, if you pay TZS 180 in VAT on raw materials, you can reclaim this amount when filing your VAT return.

Maintaining accurate records of all sales and purchases is crucial for VAT compliance. VAT returns, typically submitted monthly, summarize VAT collected on sales and VAT paid on purchases, determining your net VAT payable or refundable. VAT returns and payments are due by the 20th of the month following the tax period. If the 20th falls on a weekend or holiday, you may file on the next working day, providing flexibility to avoid penalties. Missing deadlines can lead to fines and interest on unpaid amounts, so staying on top of VAT requirements is essential.

Having the right documents ready is essential for VAT registration, allowing your business to collect VAT legally. Documentation requirements vary depending on your business structure.

For *sole proprietors,* these documents are required:
- Business license.
- Business name registration certificates (if registered with BRELA).
- Completed VAT Registration Form.
- National ID, driving license, voter ID, or passport.
- Proof of meeting registration requirements.

- TIN Certificate.

For a *partnership,* the process is similar, with additional documentation for each partner:

- Business license.
- Business name registration certificates.
- Completed VAT Registration Form.
- National ID, driving license, voter ID, or passport for each partner.
- Partnership deed.
- Partnership TIN Certificate.
- Proof of meeting registration requirements.

For a registered *company,* additional company-specific documentation is required:

- Business license.
- Certificate of incorporation.
- Company TIN Certificate.
- Completed VAT Registration Form.
- Memorandum and articles of association.
- National ID, driving license, voter ID, or passport of directors or owners.
- Proof that the company meets registration requirements.

Whichever structure your business falls under, getting your VAT Registration Certificate is a key step in ensuring you're compliant with tax laws. Make sure you have all the right documents ready, as missing information can slow things down. Once registered, you can legally collect VAT and keep your business on track.

Excise Duty Registration Certificate

If your business produces or sells specific goods like alcohol, tobacco, soft drinks, or petroleum products, excise duty registration is mandatory. Excise duty is a tax imposed on goods often considered luxury items or those potentially harmful to health or the environment. It applies to products with higher risks or those that impact society in significant ways.

To legally operate, businesses must obtain an Excise Duty Registration Certificate. This certificate allows you to produce, distribute, or sell excisable goods. Without it, you risk fines, having your goods taken away, or even a business shutdown. Registering from the start ensures your business can operate and grow without legal issues.

Capital Gain Tax (CGT) Certificate

A Capital Gains Tax (CGT) Certificate is issued to individuals or businesses that have paid tax on profits from the sale or transfer of specific assets. Capital gains tax applies to assets like real estate, shares, and other investments, and the certificate proves compliance with these tax regulations.

To calculate capital gains, subtract the asset's purchase cost from its sale price. For example, if you bought property for TZS 20 million and sold it for TZS 30 million, the gain would be TZS 10 million, and this gain would be taxed.

In Tanzania, certain capital gains are exempt from CGT:

- Residential properties owned and occupied for three or more years, with gains under TZS 15 million.
- Agricultural land valued under TZS 10 million, used for farming at least two of the last three years.
- Shares listed on the DSE held by individuals with less than 25% ownership.
- Gains from transferring mineral rights to a government entity or shares to the government through the Treasury Registrar.

Here's a quick overview of some common transactions and their respective capital gain tax rates:

Transactions	Resident Rate	Non-Resident Rate

Gain on Land or Building with cost records	10%	20%
Gain on Land or Building without cost records	3%	N/A
Petroleum or mineral rights	30%	30%
Shares or securities in resident entity	10%	20%

Figure 7.4: CGT Rates

Requirements documents for obtaining CGT Certificate differ depending on the asset type. For sale of shares, you need:

- Memorandum and article of association.
- Certificate of incorporation.
- Board resolution.
- Transfer of stock.
- Current financial statement.
- Sales agreement.
- BRELA search report (shows company status).
- Commitment bond (if not signed by authorized representatives).
- Certificate fee receipt (EFD receipt).

However, for the sales of properties, you will need to submit the following documents:

- Title or offer.
- Valuation report.
- Land forms No.:
  - 29 (notification of disposition).
  - 30 (application for approval of disposition.
  - 33 (certificate of approval of a disposition.
  - 35 (transfer of right of occupancy.
  - 38 (contract for disposition of right of occupancy).
- Sales agreement.
- Deed of gift (for gifted properties).
- Deed of exchange (for exchanged properties).
- Municipal Stamp Duty Receipt.

- Commitment bond (if not signed by authorized representatives).

Your Income Tax Obligations

Your income tax obligations depend on the type of business structure you choose when registering your business. Here's how income tax works for different business types:

For solo owner, if you are registered as a sole proprietor, your tax liability is determined by your annual turnover. In Tanzania, every sole proprietorship is subject to presumptive tax rates, which vary depending on whether or not you maintain proper business records.

Proper record-keeping can result in lower tax obligations, providing a financial incentive for sole proprietors to keep accurate documentation. Here's a breakdown of the tax structure for sole proprietors based on the annual turnover:

Annual Turnover	Not Keeping Records	Keeping Records
Where turnover does not exceed TZS 4,000,000	NIL	NIL
Where turnover exceeds TZS 4,000,000 but does not exceed TZS 7,000,000	TZS 100,000	3% of the turnover exceeding TZS 4,000,000
Where turnover exceeds TZS 7,000,000 but does not exceed 11,000,000	TZS 250,000	TZS 90,000 + 3% of the turnover exceeding TZS 7,000,000
Where turnover is between TZS 11,000,000 and TZS 100,000,000	3.5% of turnover	3.5% of turnover

Figure 7.1: Presumptive Tax Rates

If your annual turnover exceeds TZS 100,000,000 or you are involved in professional services like consulting or construction, you will need to prepare audited financial statements and file an official income return.

For a partnership, if the business is owned by multiple partners, it is not taxed as a separate legal entity. Instead, each partner pays taxes on their share of the profits. Each partner reports their share of the profits or losses on their personal tax return and is taxed based on their individual tax rate. The tax burden is shared proportionally according to each partner's share of the business profits.

This approach simplifies the process because the partnership does not need to file corporate taxes. However, each partner is responsible for ensuring they meet their personal tax filing obligations.

For companies, income tax is charged on net profits. In Tanzania, a company is subject to a corporate tax rate of 30%. This rate applies to all companies, whether they are resident in Tanzania or non-resident but earning income within Tanzania's borders.

However, there's an exciting pathway you might consider to avoid that higher rate: If you decide to list your company on the Dar es Salaam Stock Exchange (DSE) and manage to issue at least 30% of your equity ownership to the public for three consecutive years from your listing date, your company could benefit from a reduced corporate tax rate from 30% to 25%. This reduction applies to both resident and non-resident companies. Going public not only provides potential access to a broader pool of capital but can also reduce your tax burden, an attractive benefit for entrepreneurs like yourself.

Moreover, if your venture involves assembling motor vehicles, tractors, or fishing boats, you have another opportunity for tax relief. By entering into a performance agreement with the Government of the United Republic of Tanzania (URT), your newly established company could qualify for a remarkably low corporate tax rate of just 10% for the first five years from the start of production.

Other Tax Obligations You Should Know

As a business owner, you have several important tax responsibilities beyond the basics. Understanding these obligations and paying the required taxes correctly helps you avoid penalties and shows that your business is operating legally and complying with tax laws.

1. Pay As You Earn (PAYE). As an entrepreneur with employees, it's important to understand your duties under the PAYE system. This system requires you to deduct a part of your employees' monthly salaries as income tax before they receive their pay.

As the employer, it's your responsibility to send this deducted amount to the TRA every month. Below is a table showing the tax rates for employees in Tanzania Mainland and Zanzibar:

Monthly Income	Tax Rate
Where total income does not exceed TZS 270,000	NIL
Where total income exceeds TZS 270,000 but does not exceed TZS 520,000	8% of the amount exceeding TZS 270,000
Where total income exceeds TZS 520,000 but does not exceed TZS 760,000	TZS 20,000 + 20% of the amount exceeding TZS 520,000
Where total income exceeds TZS 760,000 but does not exceed TZS 1,000,000	TZS 68,000 + 25% of the amount exceeding TZS 760,000
Where total income exceeds TZS 1,000,000	TZS 128,000 + 30% of the amount exceeding TZS 1,000,000

Figure 7.2: PAYE Rates

For resident entrepreneurs who employ non-resident staff, it's important to note that the remuneration for these employees is subject to a withholding tax of 15%. Additionally, the total monthly income for non-resident employees, as well as for employees holding secondary employment, is taxed at a flat rate of 30%.

Make sure you file PAYE return and pay on time. The due date for the submission of the PAYE return and payment is on or before the *7th day of the following month.* This means that for any salary or wages paid in a particular month, the corresponding PAYE return and payment must be completed by the 7th of the next month.

2. Skills Development Levy (SDL). As an entrepreneur navigating the landscape of business in Tanzania, it's important to be aware of your obligations regarding the SDL obligations. This essential tax requires businesses to contribute 3.5% of their monthly gross emoluments if they operate in Tanzania Mainland, and 4% if they're based in Zanzibar.

The SDL is not just a tax; it's an investment in the future of your workforce. The funds collected through this levy support vital skills development initiatives and training programs that enhance the capabilities of employees across various industries. By contributing to the SDL, you're playing a key role in building a skilled labor force that meets the needs of today's competitive market.

Additionally, it's important to remember that if your business is eligible for the SDL, you are required to file an SDL return in both Tanzania Mainland and Zanzibar. The due date for the submission of the Skills Development Levy (SDL) return and payment is on or before the *7th day of the following month.* It's essential to adhere to this deadline to ensure compliance and avoid any penalties.

3. Stamp duty obligation. It's important to familiarize yourself with the stamp duty obligation that comes into play with certain legal documents. Stamp duty is a tax applied to specific transactions, often related to legal documents such as property transfers, lease agreements, and various contracts.

When starting your business, you'll likely need to secure an office space, either through ownership or leasing. If you choose to lease, be aware that the lease agreement is subject to a stamp duty of 1% on the annual rent you pay. This means that as you finalize your lease, you will need to account for this additional cost in your budget.

Return of Income

As an entrepreneur, it's essential to understand the importance of filing a return of income each year, especially if you're required to prepare an audited financial statement for your business. This document summarizes your business's total income, expenses, and taxes paid throughout the year, giving you a clear overview of its financial performance.

Submitting your return of income not only encourages transparency in financial reporting but also helps the TRA accurately assess the taxes you've paid. Remember, this return must be submitted *within six months following the end of your financial year.* For instance, if your financial year runs from January 1, 2024, to December 31, 2024, you'll need to file your return of income between January 1, 2025, and June 30, 2025.

Timely submission is crucial to avoid penalties or extra attention from the TRA. By filing your return of income on time, you not only ensure compliance with tax regulations but also maintain your business's good standing with tax authorities. This proactive approach allows your business to operate smoothly without facing legal or financial setbacks.

So, take this step seriously! Stay organized and keep track of your financial records throughout the year. By doing so, you'll position your business for success and ensure a stress-free filing process.

Statement of Your Tax Estimate

Are you conducting a self-assessment for your taxes? If so, submitting a statement of your tax estimate to the relevant tax authority is essential. This statement shows your projected income for the upcoming year along with the estimated taxes you expect to pay.

Why is this requirement so important? For the tax authority, it helps with planning and collecting revenue for the year. For you, it's a chance to take control of your tax responsibilities and keep your business compliant. By providing an accurate estimate, you can avoid the issues of underpayment or overpayment, which can affect your cash flow.

To create an accurate statement, take time to evaluate your expected profits, expenses, and other financial activities carefully. Think about any changes in your revenue or possible deductions. This careful planning will give you a clearer view of your finances.

Remember, timely and accurate submissions are key. Missing the deadline or providing incorrect information can lead to penalties, interest on unpaid taxes, or even a review by the tax authority. By staying organized in this process, you'll not only protect your business but also set it up for future success.

Installments of Income Tax Payments

As an entrepreneur, it is your legal responsibility to pay income tax on the profits generated by your business, regardless of whether you operate as a sole proprietorship, partnership, or company. The government requires that income tax be paid in four installments throughout the year.

The first installment is paid *on or before March 31st.* Consider this payment as your fresh start to the year, it's your initial opportunity to fulfill your tax obligations and set a positive tone for the months ahead. The second installment is paid *on or before June 30th.* By this time, you should have gained valuable insights into your business's performance during the first half of the year. This understanding will help you make informed decisions as you move forward.

The third installment is paid *on or before September 30th.* This is a good time to pause and look at how your business is doing as the year goes on. It's time for your final installment. It's also time for your final payment. As the year ends, make sure you submit your last payment *on or before December 31st.* This important payment will complete your tax obligations for the year, allowing you to finish your business records confidently and without worry.

Electronic Fiscal Receipts (EFD)

In Tanzania, businesses with an annual turnover of TZS 11,000,000 or more are required by law to acquire an EFD and issue electronic fiscal receipts for all transactions. These receipts are essential for tracking sales and ensuring compliance with tax regulations.

If your annual turnover is below TZS 11,000,000, while you're not mandated to use an EFD, it's still crucial to issue manual receipts. Ensure these receipts include specific details such as the full names of both the seller and buyer, their Taxpayer Identification Numbers (TINs), a description of the goods or services provided, and the buyer's address. Including these particulars helps maintain accurate records and encourages transparency in your transactions, which is particularly important for smaller businesses.

Failure to issue a fiscal receipt or providing false information on a receipt is considered a serious offense under Tanzanian tax law. Such violations can lead to significant fines that may disrupt your business operations. It is vital to comply with tax regulations by properly issuing fiscal receipts. This not only helps you avoid penalties but also positions your business for long-term success.

Tax Calculation for Your Business

Before moving on to the next chapter, take your time to think about how fulfilling it will be to open your very own bakery, registered as Tanzania Sweet Bakery. You have big dreams and delicious treats in mind, but first, you need to get a TIN certificate and a Tax Clearance Certificate to apply for your business license.

After gathering all the required documents, you walk into the local TRA office, feeling excited. After a short wait, you finally reach the tax officer's desk.

"Hello! I'd like to apply for a TIN certificate and a Tax Clearance Certificate so I can move forward with my bakery's business license," you say with a smile.

The tax officer looks up and smiles back at you. "Welcome! You're taking an important step. Let's look at your documents." They check your papers and nod with approval. "Great news: getting your TIN certificate is free! Here it is," they say, handing you the freshly printed document.

"Thank you so much! This is wonderful!" you respond, feeling a wave of happiness.

"Now, let's talk about the Tax Clearance Certificate. What is your expected annual revenue?" the officer asks, ready to help you.

"I expect to make between TZS 7,000,000 and TZS 11,000,000. I've found a nice place for my bakery that costs TZS 100,000 each month, and I've already paid TZS 600,000 upfront for the first six months as part of my lease agreement," you explain confidently.

The tax officer nods and thinks for a moment. "Based on your expected revenue and expenses, you'll need to pay TZS 134,500 for your Tax Clearance Certificate. First, let me create a payment control number for you." The officer types quickly on the computer and hands you a slip with the number printed on it. "Once you make this payment and bring back the receipt, I can give you your certificate."

"That sounds good! I really appreciate your help. I was worried about this process, but you've made it feel so easy," you reply, feeling relieved.

"I'm happy to help! Starting a business is an exciting journey, and I'm here to support you. Remember, every great bakery starts with a single loaf of bread!" the officer says cheerfully.

You both laugh together, and in that moment, all your stress goes away.

"Thank you for your encouragement! I'll make that payment today and come back with the receipt," you promise with renewed energy.

"I look forward to seeing you again! Good luck with Tanzania Sweet Bakery! You are on your way to baking something special," the officer replies with a friendly smile.

You might be wondering how the tax officer arrived at this amount. Let's break down each part of the tax calculation so you can understand clearly.

Income Tax from Annual Revenue. Since your bakery is expected to generate between TZS 7,000,000 and TZS 11,000,000 annually, you fall into a specific tax bracket. For this range, Tanzania's tax rules require an annual income tax payment of TZS 250,000, divided into four installments paid quarterly.

Quarterly Payment: TZS 250,000 ÷ 4 = TZS 62,500 every three months.

For now, you need to pay the first installment of TZS 62,500.

Stamp Duty on the Lease Agreement. Stamp duty applies to rental agreements and is calculated as 1% of the total annual rent. Since your bakery's space rents at TZS 100,000 per month, your yearly rent is:

- Annual Rent: TZS 100,000 × 12 months = TZS 1,200,000.
- Stamp Duty: TZS 1,200,000 × 1% = TZS 12,000.

Withholding Tax on the Lease Agreement. Withholding tax is another requirement for lease agreements in Tanzania, calculated as 10% of any advance rent payment. Since you paid TZS 600,000 upfront for six months, the withholding tax will be:

Withholding Tax: TZS 600,000 × 10% = TZS 60,000.

Now, to fulfill the tax requirements for your Tax Clearance Certificate, you need to sum up and pay the following amounts:

- First Income Tax Installment: TZS 62,500
- Stamp Duty: TZS 12,000
- Withholding Tax: TZS 60,000

Grand Total: TZS 62,500 + TZS 12,000 + TZS 60,000 = TZS 134,500

Once you've paid the total amount of TZS 134,500, you'll have completed the necessary tax requirements. The Tax Clearance Certificate shows that you're fully compliant with tax laws, allowing you to proceed with confidence and focus on growing your business without any legal obstacles. This essential step also reinforces the importance of tax compliance as you work toward turning your business dreams into reality.

Self-Reflection

Now, take a moment to answer the self-questions below to discover how well you have mastered tax compliance.

Questions	My Answer
1. What does tax mean for my business, and why is it important?	
2. Who handles tax matters in Tanzania for my business?	
3. Which key tax certificates do I need?	
4. What tax obligations do I have as an entrepreneur in Tanzania?	
5. When should I pay income tax, and why are the deadlines important?	
6. How does withholding tax work, and why is it necessary?	
7. How will I keep accurate financial records throughout the year?	
8. Do I have all the required tax certificates? If not, how will I get them?	
9. What happens if I don't register for VAT, but I meet the revenue threshold?	
10. Am I ready to handle tax obligations as my business grows?	

Figure 7.5: Self-Assessment Questions

Chapter 7

Acquiring Your License

"The road to business success is paved with licenses and permits. Without them, you risk your venture's foundation."

— Donald Trump

Some people think getting a business license is a mysterious journey filled with confusing signs and dead ends. But in reality, it can be a joyful path to your dreams!

In this chapter, you'll explore the risks of operating without a license and what to avoid in the application process. You'll identify the license that fits your business and learn how to obtain it.

By the end of this chapter, you'll reflect on your knowledge of the licensing process. You'll be ready to navigate the application steps, whether you're a citizen of the United Republic of Tanzania or a foreign national looking to do business in Tanzania. You'll be equipped with the knowledge needed to ensure your business operates legally and smoothly.

Business License

A business license is your business's VIP pass to the world of entrepreneurship! It's a legal ticket that lets you operate your business in a specific area, whether it's your neighborhood or a whole city. In Tanzania, having a business license is not just a rule; it's a crucial part of making your business run smoothly and helping it grow without any legal headaches. With this license, you can operate freely in your field, apply for contracts, and build important partnerships. Without a license, your business could face fines, be shut down, and risk losing its good name.

Having this license builds trust with your partners, clients, and even the government, signaling that you are running an honest and reliable business. So, getting your business license is essential. It's the official permission you need to operate and grow your business. With this important document in hand, you can confidently seek new opportunities and expand your venture.

Risks of Operating Without a License

As an entrepreneur, one of your key responsibilities is to ensure that your business operates legally at all times. This means obtaining a valid business license and keeping it up to date. Operating without a valid license can lead to unexpected challenges that you definitely want to avoid.

Let's assume that you wake up one day and find out your business is in trouble. How would you feel? Would your mind race with worry, thinking about everything you've worked for? In Tanzania, if you operate without a valid license, you could face heavy fines, restrictions, or even full investigations into your business. If the authorities discover you've been running things illegally for a long time, those penalties can become quite serious. Keeping your business license current helps you avoid these legal headaches, allowing you to focus on your passions instead. By staying compliant, you protect your dreams and enjoy the journey without the stress of unexpected setbacks.

Now, think about your favorite store. You trust it because it plays by the rules. If you found out that this store is breaking the law, would you still want to shop there? Having legal problems with your business license can hurt your reputation. Customers, partners, and investors prefer to work with businesses that follow the rules. If they find out that you're operating without a license, it could seriously damage your brand and make it hard to win back their trust. By ensuring you're compliant, you protect the good name you've worked so hard to build.

Let's say you're trying to build your dream, but suddenly a legal issue puts your personal belongings at risk. In some cases, entrepreneurs can be personally responsible for running an unlicensed business. This means that if you face legal action or financial penalties, your personal assets, like your home or savings, could be at stake. Understanding the dangers of not keeping your business license valid will help you avoid unnecessary trouble and protect both your business and yourself.

Mistakes You Must Avoid

When it comes to applying for a business license, many new entrepreneurs may think it's easy. However, they often fall into traps that can slow things down or even cause legal problems. By avoiding these common mistakes, you can save time, money, and stress. After all, you want your business to be registered correctly and follow the rules from the start, right? Let's look at some typical mistakes and share helpful tips to make getting your business license easier.

First, don't ignore the specific rules for your industry. A big mistake many entrepreneurs make is overlooking the special regulations that apply to their type of business. If you're in industries like food, mining, or healthcare, you might need additional approvals. Before you apply for your business license, take the time to understand what your industry requires. When you're clear on what's needed, you'll feel more confident and prepared to start your application!

Next, be cautious about providing incorrect or incomplete documents. Many applications get delayed or turned down due to mistakes in the information you provide. To avoid this, carefully check the list of required documents for your business license. Make sure every form is filled out correctly, and don't forget to include any extra documents, like proof of business registration or tax papers. Think of it like checking off items on a grocery list: double-check everything before you submit!

Another common error is missing application deadlines. Submitting your application late can have serious consequences, especially for license renewals. You might face fines or even be forced to close your business temporarily. To stay on top of things, set reminders for yourself and aim to submit your documents early. It's full of joy to feel stress-free, knowing your application is in on time!

Lastly, remember to follow local rules after you get your license. This means filing taxes each year, meeting industry standards, and keeping your business compliant. Ignoring these regulations can lead to penalties, fines, or even the loss of your business license. It is full of benefits, including running your business with peace of mind because you're adhering to all the rules! Being compliant allows you to focus on growing your business without worrying about unexpected legal trouble.

By avoiding these common mistakes, you can make your journey to getting a business license much smoother. Remember, you're building something great, and starting off right sets the tone for your success!

Lines of Business Schedules in Tanzania

When starting a business in Tanzania, it's important to know where your business fits in the government's list of business categories.

The government has divided businesses into two main schedules based on the type of activity, size, and industry.

1. Line of Business Schedule "A": This includes businesses that need special skills, follow more rules, and require a larger investment. These businesses are usually bigger and can significantly impact the economy, public safety, or the environment. Because of this, businesses in Schedule "A" must meet stricter requirements and follow more laws.

To apply for a business license under Schedule "A," you need to send your application to the BRELA. This agency is in charge of collecting fees and issuing licenses. The application process might involve more paperwork and require approval from different authorities to ensure your business complies with specific laws.

Here are some examples of businesses that fall under Line of Business Schedule "A":

- Any business of national or international nature or governed by policy.
- Bank and financial institution, capital market, credit card management, stock exchange and stock exchange brokers.
- Broadcasting and television.
- Bureau de exchange.
- Cargo tallying.
- Cargo valuation, cargo superintendence and Pre-shipment inspection.
- Clearing and forwarding/freight forwarders.
- Commercial traveler.
- Commission agent or manufacture representatives.
- Courier services and mail agent.
- Dealers in arms and ammunition.
- Dealers in broadcasting apparatus.
- Dealers in explosives.
- Electricity production and distribution.
- Estate agency, estate developer, property managements, real estate agent.

- Export and selling.
- Fax, telex, email, internet service provider, internet cafe, internet surfing, telecommunication service and sells of tele-communication equipment.
- Gold and silver smith and gemstone dealers.
- Harbor and cargo handling.
- Handles/miscellaneous port services.
- Import and selling.
- Insurance and Assurance, insurance broker, and re-Insurance.
- Manufacturing and selling.
- Motor vehicles dealers.
- Night club.
- Postal services.
- Refining crude oil.
- Shipping agency.
- Shipping business.
- Social security providers.
- Stevedoring or lighter-age.
- Tourist hotel, lodge, camps, tour operators, hunting safaris, travel agent, car hiring or renting, tourist photographic and tourist promotion.
- Transportation of passengers and goods by railways.
- Transportation of passengers or goods by air.
- Water drilling and supply.

2. Line of Business Schedule "B": This includes businesses that are easier and cheaper to start compared to those in Schedule "A." These businesses are usually smaller and don't pose as much risk to public safety or the environment. Because of this, the process for getting a license is simpler.

To apply for a business license under Schedule "B," you need to go to your District, Town, or Municipal Council. The licensing officers there will help you through the process, collect any fees, and issue your license. This process usually involves less paperwork. However, you will still need to provide some basic information about your business and ensure that you follow local tax laws.

Here are some examples of businesses that fall under Line of Business Schedule "B":

- Any other business which is not of national/International nature or governed/proceeded by policy.
- Attended telephone services.
- Auctioneer.
- Brokers.
- Building contractors, electrical contractors, mechanical contractors, civil workers contractors, etc.
- Co-operative societies.
- General merchandizing (super markets, department store etc.).
- Insurance agent.
- Internet trade.
- Printing and publishing of books and newspapers.
- Regional trading companies.
- Restaurants and ordinary hotels and guest houses.
- Small scale manufacturing and selling.
- Spare parts, machine tools.
- Specified professionals.
- Transportation of passengers within the city municipal and township.
- Wholesale trade.

How to Identify a Schedule That Fits You

If you want to start a business in Tanzania, it's important to find out if your business falls under Schedule "A" or Schedule "B" before applying for a business license. Knowing this helps you get your license faster and follow the right rules. Understanding the differences between these schedules is essential for ensuring that your business complies with the regulations that apply to your specific industry.

Different industries have different rules. For example, if your business is in tourism, large manufacturing, telecommunications, or finance, you need to follow stricter regulations because these areas can significantly impact public safety and the economy. If you're in one of these industries, you will likely need a Schedule "A" license, which has tougher requirements. In contrast, if your business operates in areas like retail, food services, or personal services, you may just need a Schedule "B" license. These types of businesses usually have fewer rules and an easier licensing process.

Another factor to consider is *the size of your business.* Think about how big your business will be. Large businesses that require significant investment or extensive facilities, like mining, large manufacturing, or real estate development, usually need a Schedule "A" license. This is because these businesses can greatly impact the economy and necessitate more government oversight. Conversely, smaller businesses, such as local shops, small manufacturers, or service providers, generally only need a Schedule "B" license. These smaller enterprises are considered less risky and easier to manage.

You should also take into account *the risks involved in your business.* If you're engaged in high-risk activities, such as handling dangerous chemicals, operating heavy machinery, or working with vulnerable populations, you will probably need a Schedule "A" license. These businesses require special safety measures and more government monitoring to ensure everyone's safety. On the other hand, businesses with lower risks, such as consulting, small retail, or office services, typically only need a Schedule "B" license. These types of businesses are safer and do not face as many regulatory requirements.

Lastly, consider *how your business might impact public or environmental safety.* If your business affects public health, safety, or the environment, you will need a stricter license. For instance, businesses involved in water drilling, air or railway transport, or selling explosives can have a significant impact on public and environmental safety. These businesses will most likely require a Schedule "A" license due to the higher levels of government monitoring. In contrast, lower-risk businesses, such as brokers, professional services, or department stores, usually only need a Schedule "B" license. Since these businesses do not significantly impact public safety, they are subject to fewer regulations.

Now that you understand these factors, you can easily determine which category your business fits into. This knowledge will help you move forward with your dream of becoming an entrepreneur in Tanzania!

Requirements for Obtaining a License

Obtaining a business license is essential for any business operating in Tanzania. To qualify, businesses must meet specific requirements, which vary based on factors such as the business structure, industry, location, and activities.

Getting a business license for a sole proprietorship is a straightforward process, but you will need the following documents to complete your application:

- Business registration certificate and an extract from the registrar (only if your business is registered with BRELA).
- Lease agreement (if you rent your business space).
- Proof of citizenship, such as a copy of your National ID, voter card, birth certificate, or passport.
- Residence permit (for foreigners).
- Specific business permit (if your business needs a permit from the relevant authority or ministry).
- Tax clearance certificate.
- TIN certificate.
- Working permit (for foreigners).

If you want to apply for a business license for a partnership, you will need to provide more documents than you would for a sole proprietorship. Here are the key documents required for a partnership license application:

- Business registration certificate and an extract from the registrar of partnership businesses.
- Lease agreement (if you rent your business space).
- Partnership deed (optional, but it can be helpful).
- Proof of citizenship for each partner, such as a copy of the National ID, voter card, birth certificate, or passport.
- Residence permits for each partner (for foreigners).
- Specific business permit (if your partnership needs a permit from the relevant authority or ministry).
- Tax clearance certificate for the partnership.
- TIN certificate for the partnership.
- Working permit for each partner (for foreigners).

If you want to establish a company, you need to provide specific documents to meet the licensing requirements. Here are the key documents you will need:

- Certificate of incorporation.
- Lease agreement (if you rent your business space).
- Memorandum and articles of association (these outlines how your company operates).
- Proof of citizenship for each director and owner, such as a copy of the National ID, voter card, birth certificate, or passport.
- Residence permits for each director and owner (for foreigners).
- Specific business permit (if your company needs a permit from the relevant authority or ministry).
- Tax clearance certificate for the company.
- TIN certificate for the company.

- Working permit for each director and owner (for foreigners).

Once you've gathered all the necessary documents for your business, the next step is to calmly submit your application to the right authority. Take a moment to carefully double-check everything to ensure your documents are accurate and up-to-date. You wouldn't want any missing or incorrect information to slow things down or cause any issues, would you? Everything will fall into place smoothly when you ensure it's all in order!

Permits to Get a Business License

In Tanzania, certain industries are closely watched because they can impact public health, safety, and the environment. Because of this, businesses in these areas need special permits or approvals in addition to a regular business license. These permits ensure that businesses follow important laws and regulations, including those that protect the environment and public health. Here are some common special business permits you may need to consider when applying for your business license in Tanzania:

- *Air Worthiness Certificate and Permit.* This is required from the Tanzania Civil Aviation Authority (TCAA) for air transportation services, including charter flights and aerial work.
- *Ammunition Dealers License.* This is required from the Tanzania Police and Defense Force (TPDF) for businesses dealing in firearms and ammunition.
- *Banking and Financial Institution Licenses.* This is needed from the Bank of Tanzania (BOT) for banks, currency exchange businesses, and microfinance institutions.
- *Capital Exchange and Stock Licenses.* This is obtained from the Capital Market and Security Authority (CMSA) for stockbrokers.

- *Crop Board Permit.* This is needed from respective Crop Boards for businesses dealing with agricultural products like cashew, tea, coffee, and more.
- *Customs Agency License (CAL).* This is required from the TRA for businesses in clearing and forwarding goods, bonded warehouses, and container depots.
- *Electricity License.* This is required from the Energy and Water Utility Regulatory Authority (EWURA) for businesses involved in electricity production and supply.
- *Explosive Dealers License.* This is needed for businesses providing explosive services to mining companies, also issued by the Ministry of Minerals and Energy.
- *Export Permit.* This is obtained from the Ministry of Agriculture, Livestock, and Fisheries for businesses exporting agricultural products.
- *Gaming License.* This is issued by the Gaming Board of Tanzania for businesses operating casinos, lotteries, and other gaming activities.
- *Industrial License.* This is required from the Business Registration and Licensing Agency (BRELA) for businesses involved in manufacturing and processing in various industries.
- *Insurance License.* This is issued by the Tanzania Insurance Regulatory Authority (TIRA) for businesses like insurance companies, brokers, and agents.
- *Land Transport License.* This is needed from the Surface and Marine Transportation Regulatory Authority (SUMATRA) for businesses involved in transporting goods and passengers by road and rail.
- *Medicine and Medical Devices Permit.* This is issued by the Tanzania Medicine and Medical Device Authority (TMDA) for businesses dealing with drugs, medical devices, cosmetics, and food products.

- *Merchant License.* This is issued by the Tanzania Ports Authority (TPA) for businesses providing port services and ship supplies.
- Mining Licenses. This is granted by the Ministry of Minerals and Energy for businesses engaged in mineral exploration and mining activities.
- *Petroleum Dealers License.* This is also issued by EWURA for businesses refining and selling petroleum products.
- *Professional Certificate.* This is required from the relevant Professional Boards for businesses offering specialized services, such as engineering, accounting, auditing, taxation, healthcare, and legal services.
- *Shipping License.* This is obtained from the Tanzania Shipping Agencies Corporation (TASAC) for shipping companies and related services.
- *Telecommunication and Broadcasting Licenses.* This is required from the Tanzania Communication Regulatory Authority (TCRA) for businesses involved in telecommunication services, postal services, radio and TV broadcasting, and internet services.
- *Tourist Agency License (TAL).* This is required from the Ministry of Tourism and Natural Resources for businesses such as tourist hotels, lodges, travel agencies, car rentals, and safari operators.
- *Water Dealers License.* This is required from EWURA for businesses producing and supplying water.
- *Water Drilling Permit.* This is needed from the Ministry of Water and Irrigation for businesses involved in water drilling and supply.

Digital Licensing Systems in Tanzania

One of the positive changes in Tanzania's business environment is the government's move toward digital licensing systems. The launch of online business licensing portals has changed how entrepreneurs apply for licenses. By offering these services online, the government has made it easier for entrepreneurs to access important information from anywhere in the country, reducing the need to visit government offices in person.

If you need to get a business license under Schedule "A", you can use the licensing portal at *https://business.go.tz*. This portal is connected to the BRELA, and the licensing officers of this government agency use this site to issue your license.

For a business license under Schedule "B", you should use the portal at *https://tausi.tamisemi.go.tz*. This site is linked to the President's Office Regional Administration and Local Government (PO-RALG) or TAMISEMI. The local municipal council where your business is located uses this portal to process your license.

These online licensing systems in Tanzania make the licensing process not only faster but also clearer. As an entrepreneur, you can track the status of your applications and quickly solve any problems that arise. As Tanzania continues to improve its licensing systems, it is expected that even more services will become available online, making the process easier for entrepreneurs.

How to Apply for a Schedule "A" License

If your business falls under Schedule "A," you can obtain a business license online at *https://business.go.tz*. Follow these steps to get started, and ensure you have all the necessary documents ready for a smooth process.

1. Register Your Account. First, visit the business license application platform at *https://business.go.tz* and click on "Login." You'll see a "Register" button; go ahead and click that. Next, fill in the required information, such as:

- Email address.
- Gender.
- Mobile phone number.
- Password.

- Your name.

Once you've entered everything, click "Register." Congratulations! You've just created your account.

2. Log in to Your Account. Now that your account is set up, log in using your email as your username and the password you created. Look for the menu on the website and click on "Services." From there, select "Business Licensing Services" to proceed.

3. Select Your Business Type and License. Once you're on the business licensing services page, scroll down to find the option to select your business type. You can choose from options like individual (for sole proprietorship), partnership, limited company, limited liability company, or foreign corporation, whatever best fits your business structure. Next, select the sector, category, and the type of business license you need. After that, click "Apply for Business License."

4. Fill Applicant Information. This section is for you as the applicant, whether it's you or a representative. You'll need to provide the following information:

- Address details (region, district, ward, village, street, mobile number, and email).
- Date of birth.
- Nationality (citizen or foreign).
- Your name.

5. Fill Business Details. Here, you will need to enter important information about your business:

- Business address details (region, district, ward, village, street, mobile number, email, plot number, block number, and office building number).
- Business name.
- Number of directors or partners, along with their names.
- Number of shareholders.
- Registration number or certificate of incorporation.
- Share percentage (if applicable).
- Shareholders' citizenship.

- TIN number.

6. Upload the Required Documents. Now it's time to attach the necessary documents based on your business structure. To know which documents you need, refer to the licensing requirements for sole proprietorships, partnerships, and companies that we discussed earlier in this chapter. Upload them all and move forward to the next part.

7. Make a Declaration. Here, you'll see a box to tick that confirms the information you provided is correct and complete to the best of your knowledge. Once you check that box, click "Apply," and then wait for feedback from the licensing officer.

8. Pay for the Business License Fee. If everything looks good, a licensing officer will send you an email with payment information for your business license fee. After making the payment, confirm it by going to "My Dashboard" and selecting "My Task." You'll find a task for your application there. Click the down arrow on the right side and select "Paid."

If you don't receive the payment information, you might get a correction inquiry via email, asking you to make changes to your application. You can find it in "My Task," make the necessary corrections, and resubmit your application.

9. Download Your License. Once your license is approved, you'll receive an email notification. Log in to your account, go to "My Dashboard," and select "My License." You'll see the details of your business license, along with an "Actions" button. Click this button, and you'll find the option to download your license.

How to Apply for a Schedule "B" License

If your business falls under Schedule 'B,' you can submit your application for a business license online at *https://tausi.tamisemi.go.tz.* The following steps will guide you through the entire process. Make sure you have all the necessary documents ready beforehand to simplify the process.

1. Create Your Account. visit the business license application platform at *https://tausi.tamisemi.go.tz* and click on "Create Account." You will see two options to create your account. You can either answer questions based on the information you used when applying for your NIDA number or receive a one-time password (OTP) sent to your registered mobile number.

Choose the method that works best for you. Both options will require you to enter your NIDA number and mobile number. If you choose to answer questions, you'll fill in your personal information and create a password for your account. If you go with the OTP option, you will receive an OTP to enter, followed by your personal information and password. Once you finish, your account will be set up!

2. Log in to Your Account. After creating your account, log in using your NIDA number as your username and the password you just created. Keep in mind, only individuals with a NIDA number can create an account and apply for licenses, whether for a sole proprietorship, partnership, or company. If you are applying for a company license, you need to be a company representative. You must first send an application letter to your local municipal council to get approval as a representative.

3. Select Your Business Area. Once you are logged in, go to your account dashboard and click on "Business License." Next, click on the button labeled "New Business License." Here, you will fill out details about your business area, including your region and Local Government Authority. After completing this section, click "Next" to continue.

4. Fill in the License Details. At this stage, choose "Principal License" if this is your first license or "Subsidiary License" if you're applying for a branch or a second license. You will need to provide the following information:

- Business address (street, ward, block number, and plot number).
- Business license type and category.
- Desired license period.

- Name of your business.

Once you've filled out these details, click "Next" to move forward.

5. Attach the Required Documents. Now, it's time to attach the necessary documents based on your business structure. To find out what documents you need, review the licensing requirements for sole proprietorships, partnerships, and companies that we discussed earlier.

6. Submit Your Application. After attaching all required documents, click the "Submit" button. Wait for about two or three days for processing.

7. Pay the Business License Fee. Within three days, you will receive payment details for your business license fee. The fee varies based on the type of license. If you don't see any updates, log back into your account. On your dashboard, find the business license section and click "View." Here, you'll see your application along with options to check the progress, view your bill, or edit your application.

To view the payment details, click the bill symbol. If it says "No Bill Found," it means your payment has not yet been generated, or there may be an issue with your application. In that case, contact your local municipal council for assistance.

8. Download Your License. Once you've paid the license fee, you'll receive a confirmation message on your mobile phone. This message will let you know that your payment was successful and your license is being processed. Log in to your account again, go to the business license section on your dashboard, and you can either print or download your business license from there.

Licensing Process for Foreign Investors

Are you a foreign investor ready to make your mark in Tanzania? What a thrilling adventure awaits! Understanding the licensing process is the first step on this amazing journey. While you will follow many of the same guidelines as Tanzanian citizens, there are some special rules for foreign investors that will help you succeed.

To kick things off, you will need to apply for a work permit and a residence permit. But wait, there's more! You can also apply for an investment certificate through the Tanzania Investment Centre (TIC). This valuable opportunity opens up a world of benefits for you, including tax incentives and smoother access to licenses. It's like having a helpful guide who ensures that your rights as an investor are protected under Tanzanian law.

If your heart is set on investing in the beautiful Zanzibar, make sure to reach out to the Zanzibar Investment Promotion Authority (ZIPA). They offer fantastic support just like TIC does on the mainland, making it even easier for you to navigate your investment journey.

Work Permits for Foreigners

Tanzania is a colorful place full of chances and rich culture. Whether you want to start a business or share your skills, the right work permit helps you reach your dreams. Tanzania offers five types of work permits, classified as A, B, C, D, and E, each tailored to suit your unique journey. You can apply for your work permit at *https://epermit.kazi.go.tz*.

Work Permit Class A is perfect for dreamers ready to start their own business in Tanzania, with a fee of $1,000. Class B is for professionals like doctors, oil and gas experts, and teachers in science and math, requiring a fee of $500. This opens doors to meaningful work and lets you make a difference in the community.

Class C is for those in other professions, also costing $1,000, allowing you to share your skills and impact lives. Class D is for individuals involved in approved religious or charitable work, with a fee of $500, helping you spread kindness. Finally, Class E is free for refugees, ensuring everyone can build a life in Tanzania and contribute to a diverse, welcoming society!

Before applying for any work permit, gather these important documents:

- A copy of a valid passport (make sure it's valid for at least six months) (for all classes).
- A detailed curriculum vitae or resume (for class B, C, D, and E).
- Certificate of charitable organization or related document (for class D).
- Certificate of incorporation or compliance for companies, NGOs, etc. (for all classes).
- Certificate of tax identification number (for all classes).
- Certificate of value-added tax (for all classes).
- Current proof of shares from the BRELA Online Search System or extract from the register (for class A).
- Current tax clearance certificate (for all classes).
- Detailed job description (for class B, C, D, and E).
- Employment or engagement contract (for class B, C, D, and E).
- Industrial, business, or operating license (for all classes).
- Introduction letter authorizing the employee to apply (for all classes).
- Justification letter (required for all classes).
- Lease agreement, certificate of occupancy, or title deed (for class A).
- Memorandum and articles of association or constitution (for all classes).
- One recent passport-sized photo with a blue background (for all classes).
- Original work permit (for renewals or changes).
- Proof of registration with NSSF and WCF (for all classes).

- Proof of transfer or sale of shares, including a tax clearance certificate (for class A).
- Recommendation letter from the relevant government authority (for classes B, C, and E).
- Relevant sectoral approvals or permits (for all classes), such as TMDA, TBS, ERB, NBAA, TCAA, CRB, LATRA, TASAC, and the Ministry of Education, Science and Technology. These documents ensure that you meet the specific requirements of your profession and contribute to the local regulations.
- Scanned copies of original academic or professional certificates (for classes B, C, and E).
- TIC/EPZA Certificate (where applicable). This certificate helps confirm your investment or business activities in Tanzania, and it is required for classes A, B, and C.
- Translated documents and scanned copies of certificates before translation (for class B, C, D, and E).

Residence Permits for Foreigners

Once you have your work permit as a foreigner, the next important step is applying for your residence permit! Surely, waking up each day in a beautiful country, surrounded by warm, welcoming people and rich culture, it's like living in paradise, isn't it? The residence permit opens up a world of opportunities, allowing you to truly embrace and enjoy life in Tanzania in the best way possible.

There are three types of residence permits: Class A, Class B, and Class C. To kick off your application, open your browser and visit the immigration website *(https://eservices.immigration.go.tz)*. Choose "Residence Permit Application." Creating an account is quick and easy, and soon you'll be on your way to making this wonderful place your long-term home.

Class A is perfect for those who want to invest in Tanzania. Whether you're a talented artist, a diaspora investor, or someone with a vision for a specific industry, this permit is designed for you. Class B caters to individuals with unique skills that are hard to find in the local job market. If you have specialized qualifications or are working on important projects with the government or private companies, this permit is your ticket. It recognizes your talents and the value you bring to Tanzania, helping you thrive in your profession.

Class C covers those who may not fit into Classes A or B but still have important reasons to be in Tanzania. This includes researchers, retirees, volunteers, or people attending medical treatments. Each type of permit showcases the rich diversity of stories and journeys in this beautiful country, highlighting how every individual contributes to the vibrant tapestry of life in Tanzania.

Fees vary based on the type of permit and the sector or occupation. For EAC citizens, fees range from $100 to $250, for diaspora individuals from $0 to $300, and for non-EAC citizens from $500 to $3,000. It's also important to remember that there is an additional application fee of $50 for each permit.

When applying for a residence permit in Tanzania, gathering the correct documents is crucial. Here's a unified list of requirements to help you navigate your journey more easily:

- A copy of the applicant's passport (valid for at least six months) (for all classes).
- Any other documents or requirements as directed by the Commissioner General of Immigration (for all classes).
- Certificate of incorporation, certificate of compliance, certificate of registration, or business name registration (for all classes).
- TIN certificate (for all classes).
- Certified copies of academic certificates (for Class B).
- Clearance from the Tanzania Refugee Services Department for a refugee investor (for Class A).
- Covering letter from the institution (for Class C).

- Current immigration status of other shareholders (for Class A).
- Current immigration status of the applicant (for all classes).
- Current proof of directors and shareholders of the company from BRELA/ZBPRA (for all classes).
- Curriculum vitae of the employee (for Class B).
- Dully filled online application (for all classes).
- Application letter (for all classes).
- Employment contract (for Class B and Class C).
- Enrollment process (for all classes).
- Evidence of capital and financial statement for replacement (for Class A).
- Job description for the expatriate/employee (for Class B).
- Letter of no objection if the applicant has shifted from another company (for all classes).
- National passport of dependents, if any (for all classes).
- Official translation of documents or certificates if written in languages other than English or Swahili (for Class B).
- Organization structure of the company (for Class B).
- Passport-size photograph (for all classes).
- Physical Verification Visit Report (PVV) where necessary (for all classes).
- Previous original permit in case of renewal or replacement (for all classes).
- Refugee Status Identification for a refugee investor (for Class A).
- Registration certificates from relevant authorities (if the business requires authorization) (for Class A).
- Tax clearance certificate (for all classes).
- Valid business license (for all classes).
- Work permit issued by the Labour Commissioner (Tanzania Mainland and Zanzibar) (for all classes).

Certificate of Incentive

Just because you're investing in Tanzania doesn't mean you're on your own. With the Certificate of Incentive from the government through the Tanzania Investment Centre (TIC), a world of support is at your fingertips. This certificate, established under the Tanzania Investment Act of 1997, opens doors to exciting investment opportunities and offers tax exemptions that enhance your profits. It boosts your business's credibility, simplifies the permit process with TIC's assistance, and makes financing more accessible. Plus, it connects you to a network of other businesses, allowing you to contribute to local growth by creating jobs and supporting the economy. To get this certificate, simply visit the TIC website *(https://onestopshop.tic.go.tz)* and apply for your certificate.

For local Mining and Petroleum investors, unlocking the Certificate of Incentives is now even more accessible! With a minimum investment of only $50,000, this certificate is within reach, provided the project is fully owned by Tanzanian citizens. Previously, the threshold stood at $100,000, making this recent reduction a fantastic opportunity for Tanzanian investors to step into exciting ventures more easily.

Foreign Mining and Petroleum investors, on the other hand, must have a minimum project investment valued at $500,000. This investment can be either fully foreign-owned or developed as a joint venture with Tanzanian investors.

For Strategic Investors, those contributing to especially high-impact sectors, the minimum investment capital is higher. Foreign strategic investors are required to invest at least $50,000,000, while local strategic investors need to invest a minimum of $20,000,000. This level of commitment is tailored to projects that aim to make a substantial positive impact in Tanzania, driving progress and sustainable growth.

The application process is straightforward, with a fee of $1,100. To ensure your application goes smoothly, gather the following documents:

- A covering letter that includes and attaches all the above documents
- Certified copy of the certificate of company incorporation
- Company board resolution to register the project with TIC
- Completed TIC application form (provided by the Centre)
- Copy of the company's Memorandum and Articles of Association
- Detailed business plan for your project
- Evidence of sufficient financial capital for project implementation
- Proof of project location

Business License Renewal Compliance

Once you have your business license, your work isn't over yet. Most licenses need to be renewed each year. Renewing your license is crucial to keep your business running legally. If you miss the renewal deadline, you might face fines or even have to stop your business activities.

To avoid any issues, keep track of when your license needs to be renewed and start the renewal process early. Some licenses may require new documents or inspections, depending on your type of business. Staying on top of your renewal helps you avoid unnecessary stress and keeps your business moving forward!

Self-Reflection

Use a few minutes to respond to the questions below and determine if you're ready to apply your business license.

Questions	My Answer
1. Do I need a license for my business?	
2. Is my business under Schedule "A" or "B" in Tanzania?	
3. What licensing requirements apply to my business?	
4. What mistakes must I avoid in the licensing process?	
5. Am I ready to renew my license each year?	
6. As a foreign investor, do I know the extra steps needed in Tanzania?	
7. How does my business impact safety, the environment, or industry rules?	
8. What risks are there if I run my business without a license?	
9. What should I prepare before applying for the Certificate of Incentives?	
10. What's my step toward getting my business license?	

Figure 8.1: Self-Assessment Questions

Ticket 3

Establishing Your Presence

Chapter 8

Branding and Marketing

"In today's world, a strong brand is more important than ever, and it's the marketing strategy that brings that brand to life."

— Richard Branson

Branding is the magic behind your dream business, while marketing is the powerful tool that brings it to life. Together, they create a story that builds trust and attracts loyal customers who feel connected to what you offer.

In this chapter, you'll dive into the transformative power of marketing for your brand and uncover key elements of effective brand marketing. You'll also learn strategies to make your brand stand out and explore how branding and marketing work hand in hand to help you achieve your goals.

By the end, you'll be equipped to measure your brand's performance and evaluate yourself on the concepts covered in this chapter to confidently build an engaging and impactful presence for your brand.

Branding

The spell of your business success begins with branding. It's the magic that helps people remember your business and feel connected to it. Every part of your brand, like your logo, colors, words, values, and how you talk to customers, works together like special ingredients in a secret recipe, creating something truly special.

Imagine a man who meets a woman who catches his attention completely. From the moment they see each other, something feels special. Her smile lights up the room, and her laughter sounds like a lovely song that draws him in. Everything about her, from the way she moves to the kindness in her voice, leaves a lasting impression. He thinks about her long after they part ways, feeling a strong connection he can't fully explain.

This is how a strong brand works. Just like that unforgettable woman, a good brand grabs people's attention and touches their hearts. It's not just about how things look; it's about the feelings and memories it creates. A great brand makes people want to know more, building trust and loyalty that keeps them coming back, just like the man who can't stop thinking about the woman who stole his heart. Your brand can create that same magic, inviting others to be part of your story.

As you start your branding journey, remember that every choice you make today will shape the future of your business. Every detail matters, from the words in your marketing to how you treat your customers. Don't overlook the small things, they are the pieces that come together to make your brand unique and memorable.

Marketing

Now that you've built your brand, an amazing one that can truly change lives, how do you make sure everyone hears about it? This is where marketing comes into play. It's the powerful tool that gets people talking, making them think, "Could this brand be the one I've been waiting for?" It grabs their interest and encourages them to be part of your journey.

Marketing is not just about pushing your products or services; it's about sharing something so exciting and valuable that people feel proud to be part of it. With great marketing, you're not just attracting customers; you're building a community of loyal supporters who believe in your vision and are excited to see where you'll go next.

In today's world, marketing is even more powerful because of social media. It allows you to connect directly with your audience, showing them what makes your business unique. Each post, update, or interaction is a chance to share something fresh, engage with your followers, and make them feel involved. The more you engage, the deeper your audience's connection to your business becomes, turning them into invested fans who want to see your success unfold.

The Power of Marketing for Your Brand

Look at the brands you love. What makes them stand out? It's often the way they make you feel connected. That's the heart of marketing: building relationships and creating a story that others want to join. Marketing is not only about telling people to buy, but also about inviting them into your brand's world and sharing the passion behind your products or services. When you approach marketing this way, you're not just selling; you're creating an experience.

First, People need to know your brand exists. Marketing helps make your brand known. If no one knows about your brand, they can't support it! Using creative ideas, fun videos, or showing what happens behind the scenes can help people remember your brand. When they see your brand often, it starts to feel familiar and trusted, like a friend they can count on.

Then, there's the power of trust. Trust is your secret key that keeps customers coming back for more. Marketing helps you build that trust. Share positive reviews from happy customers, show the world what your brand stands for, and be real about your values. When people trust you, they'll choose you every time. It's like building a friendship, people stick around when they know they can rely on you. So be genuine, share the love, and watch your loyal fans grow!

Marketing helps shape your brand's identity by giving it a personality! Now, interpret your brand as a person. How would they dress, speak, or act? The colors, logo, and style all create a picture in people's minds. If you stay consistent with this look, people will recognize your brand right away, whether online or in a store. It's like when you see a friend across the room, you instantly know it's them, even before they say a word.

Marketing is powerful when it truly connects with your audience. Through it, you learn exactly what they need, what they dream about, and the challenges they face. When you listen and understand them, your message becomes personal. It's like speaking their language, tapping into their hearts. When your marketing is that genuine, your audience will feel like they're part of your brand's family, and that's when the magic happens. They'll trust you, spread your message, and become your most loyal supporters!

And yes, marketing brings sales to your brand. When people connect with your brand, trust it, and see its value, they're more likely to buy from you. But it's not just about the numbers, it's about building a brand that people genuinely love and remember. When you invest in marketing, you're growing those connections, making your brand stronger, and creating a loyal group of supporters who truly believe in what you do. Sales will follow, but loyalty is what keeps your brand growing!

Elements for Effective Brand Marketing

It all starts with your brand's identity. Your logo, colors, and the message that makes people recognize you right away. Think of Pepsi's blue logo in a busy place. That blue is more than a color; it's a reminder of good times shared with friends, of happiness in a bottle. When your brand feels familiar and strong, people will think of you every time they see it. Build your brand well, and people will remember you with a positive feeling, just like they remember their best memories.

And then there's the magic of getting the word out through public relations. Assume someone tells you about an amazing new movie; that excitement spreads, and suddenly, you want to watch it too! Positive attention around your brand creates that same excitement. Connecting with bloggers, influencers, and media is like spreading this joy, reaching even more people. When your brand gets good mentions or is talked about by someone trusted, it boosts your image and makes people feel confident about choosing you.

Content creation brings your brand to life through storytelling. Think of Betty Crocker, a brand that's famous for baking, posting a video of a cake coming together, layer by layer. It's fun, it's useful, and it builds a bond with anyone who loves baking. Sharing engaging stories, tips, and updates turns your brand into a trusted friend. People see your expertise, and they come back because they enjoy what you're sharing. Just like how Betty Crocker connects with people through every recipe and baking tip, you can also create lasting connections by sharing valuable, relatable content that makes your brand feel like a friend.

Social media is where all these elements come together, like a lively marketplace full of ideas and energy. Start by choosing the platform where your audience spends time. If they are on Instagram, post bright photos that catch their attention. Show up often by replying to comments, posting regularly, and keeping things engaging. Make your page a place they enjoy visiting, where they feel valued, included, and eager to return. This way, you are not just posting but building a welcoming and lasting community.

Just as every guest has a different path to your party, each marketing channel acts as a way to bring people to your brand. Some channels are digital, like social media or emails, while others are more traditional, like print ads or events. Finding the right mix is like creating an effective approach to reach the hearts of different people who may be interested in what you offer.

Every time someone interacts with your brand, they're shaping their experience with you. Whether it's a quick response to a question or a smooth website visit, each moment counts. If someone browses your site and easily finds what they need, it builds a positive impression and makes them feel good about choosing you. These happy experiences turn into loyal customers who love sharing their positive interactions with others.

Sometimes, email marketing feels like sending a personalized note with an offer just for the recipient, like a discount on something they'll enjoy. A well-crafted email makes the reader feel seen and understood, showing that you're paying attention to their needs and preferences. It's not just about selling something, but about building a connection. When the message feels thoughtful and relevant, people appreciate it and begin to look forward to future emails. By offering value and showing you care, you keep the relationship strong and encourage loyalty.

When all these elements come together, they form a powerful story that goes beyond just marketing. It's about building lasting relationships. Your brand identity, content, public relations (PR), social media, customer experience, and email marketing all play a part in shaping how people feel about you. They help create a consistent, positive image that resonates with your audience. By crafting each piece thoughtfully and making sure it connects with the right people, you don't just attract new customers. You create loyal fans who feel valued, heard, and excited to engage with your brand again and again.

How to Make Your Brand Stand Out

Once you understand each element of brand marketing, it's time to make your brand stand out in the real world. To make this possible, you need to bring energy and purpose to it. Little by little, your brand will grow into something people trust, know, and want to be part of.

Start by giving your brand a personality. This means defining values, traits, and a purpose that will guide your brand through its journey. Ask yourself: What does your brand represent? What principles drive its actions? When your brand has a clear identity, it becomes like a person that people can connect with, relate to, and recognize easily.

Next, craft a story for your brand. Just like any great tale, your brand needs a unique journey. This could be about the challenges it solves or the positive impact it makes on people's lives. Your brand's story should capture attention, stay with people, and make your brand unforgettable.

Understanding your audience is key. You need to know who your customers are and what matters to them. What do they love? What problems do they face? Knowing these details helps you create experiences that resonate with them and make them feel like your brand was made specifically for them. It's about building a real connection by focusing on what they care about most.

Now, focus on what sets your brand apart. Every brand has something special that keeps the audience interested. It could be the way you do things, a unique feature, or a promise that only you keep. This is what differentiates your brand, making it easy for people to see why they should choose you over others.

When it comes to marketing, think of each platform like social media, emails, or ads as a stage where your brand's story comes to life. Choose the platforms your audience loves the most and use them to keep your story engaging and interactive. This will allow your brand to stay connected with people in a way that feels natural.

Every piece of content, whether it's a funny post or a thoughtful email, should stay true to your brand's voice and personality. It's important that all your messages, whether it's a tweet, an Instagram story, or a blog post, sound like they're coming from the same character. Keeping this consistency will help people stay familiar with your brand and feel involved in its journey.

As you start getting feedback from your audience, take time to notice what they enjoy most and where they are most active. Think of this feedback as chapters in a book, helping you adjust and keep the story fresh and exciting. This ensures your brand continues to engage and spark interest.

Lastly, your loyal customers become part of your brand's family. They're not just followers; they're supporters who have joined you on the journey. Make sure they feel heard and valued by giving them opportunities to share their opinions, offer feedback, and participate in your story. Over time, these customers will become a community that looks forward to every new chapter of your brand's adventure.

Branding and Marketing Interrelationship

Branding and marketing are like best friends working together to make a business unforgettable. Branding is the magic behind your business. It's what makes your business stand out, like the logo, the colors, the way you speak to your customers, and everything that shows who you are. It's like the foundation of a house because, without a solid foundation, nothing can stand tall and strong. Branding gives your business its identity and makes people remember it. When done right, branding tells the world exactly what your business is about.

Marketing, on the other hand, is what spreads that magic. It's the tool that takes your brand story and shouts it to the world. Marketing gets the word out, saying, "This is who we are, and this is why we're awesome!" Through ads, social media posts, emails, and more, marketing tells your brand's story and brings it to life in front of people. It's like making the story reach every corner, inviting people in to learn more about your business.

Together, branding and marketing are like a team of expert witches. Branding creates the message, while marketing makes sure everyone hears it, no matter what. For example, if your brand cares about being environmentally friendly, marketing will share stories about your eco-friendly products and practices. Each time marketing shares these stories, more people get to know your brand, trust it, and choose it, which helps your business grow.

The relationship between branding and marketing is a close one. Branding helps marketing understand how to talk to people. If your brand is all about luxury, marketing will focus on beautiful visuals and messages that show how special your products or services are. Both branding and marketing work together in a cycle, each one supporting the other to build excitement and trust.

When you get both of these working together, your business becomes stronger. You create growth, build loyalty, and leave a lasting impression that people won't forget. So, if you want to make your business truly stand out, remember: branding is the magic that makes your business unique, and marketing is the powerful tool that gets the world to see it. Keep that duo strong, and success will follow.

Measure Your Brand's Success

To measure your brand's success, you need to create an attractive story. Alright, let's think of your business brand as the hero in a thrilling movie. The story starts with an idea, and your brand plays a leading role, moving through different chapters. But just like any hero, you need to know: Is my brand winning the hearts of the audience? Are people cheering for my hero, or are they still unsure about whether it's going to save the day? Let's dive into how you can measure your brand's success and see how it's doing on this epic adventure!

The first step is to see how many people recognize your brand and are talking about it. This is like when your hero walks onto the stage and the audience starts cheering. This is brand awareness in action. Are people aware of your brand? Are they discussing it on social media? You can measure this by tracking social media mentions, reviewing survey results, or analyzing the number of visitors to your website. The more people engage with your brand, the more you know it's gaining attention. If you're not hearing cheers yet, don't worry. Heroes need time to build a fanbase!

Now, we're going a little deeper. Brand awareness is great, but how do people really feel about your hero? Are they excited, inspired, or moved by your story? Brand perception is the emotions your audience feels when they think about your business. This can be measured by reading reviews, asking your customers directly, or paying attention to how they talk about you. Also, loyal customers are like those die-hard fans who show up at every premiere. When people return for more, it's a sure sign that you're doing something right. Your hero's charm is working!

Okay, let's check out the action scene! View your sales performance as a way of tracking how the hero's journey is progressing. Are sales growing? Is your brand gaining more market share? High sales and growth are signs that your hero is winning the audience, taking on challenges, and collecting more fans along the way. Sales numbers provide a clear overview of your brand's journey. If your hero's story is interesting, your audience will want to invest in it (or in your product!).

Think of social media as the stage where your hero gets to shine. Social media engagement shows if people are enjoying your content and connecting with your hero. High engagement means your audience is not just watching, they're participating. They're liking, commenting, and sharing your content with their friends. It's like your hero having a parade with thousands of fans following them, cheering them on. More engagement equals more fans, and more fans mean your story is spreading.

Now, this is the most important measure of success. Brand reputation can be viewed as the hero's image. It's the trust, quality, and deep connection people have with your brand. It's how your audience feels about you over time. When people think of your brand, do they smile? Do they trust that your hero will deliver on their promises? Building a strong reputation takes time, but it's what makes your hero legendary. When your audience feels that deep connection, they'll stick with your brand even when a new hero comes to town.

To sum it all up, measuring your brand's success can be seen as tracking your hero's journey. You look at awareness (is your hero getting noticed?), perception (how do people feel about your hero?), loyalty (do they keep coming back?), sales (is your hero gaining followers?), engagement (is your hero's story going viral?), and reputation (what's your hero's image?). Each of these elements reveals important insights that help you understand your brand's growth and impact. All these pieces together give you the full view of your brand's adventure.

Create a Lasting Impact

In a world full of businesses, building a brand that connects with people is what makes it stand out. Branding and marketing are like the roots of a strong tree that help your business grow and build trust with customers. Sharing your story in the same way everywhere, on your website, social media, or ads, helps people understand and remember your brand.

The real magic happens when you listen to your customers. When you hear what they like or don't like, you can make changes that show you care about their needs. Checking how your brand is doing also helps you see where to grow and make improvements. Building a brand takes time, creativity, and the courage to try new things. But when you do it right, your brand can shine, leaving a mark that people remember for years.

Self-Reflection

Now, focus on the following self-assessment to evaluate how well you understand branding and marketing.

Questions	My Answer
1. What is the importance of branding for me in today's business world?	
2. How does marketing help bring my brand to life?	
3. What key elements contribute to my brand identity?	
4. Why is consistency important for my branding?	
5. How can I use social media effectively for my marketing?	
6. What role does public relations play in my brand marketing?	
7. How can I measure my brand awareness?	
8. What does brand perception reveal about my business?	
9. What is the relationship between my branding and marketing?	
10. How does building my brand relate to telling my story?	

Figure 9.1: Self-Assessment Questions

Chapter 9

Launching Your Business

"The only way to make a big impact is to launch your business with passion and persistence."

— Jeff Bezos

Congratulations! You're no longer just dreaming about a business; you are now the CEO, the leader of something real that you've built from the ground up. Thanks to the skills and knowledge you've gained about branding and marketing in the last chapter, it's time to open the doors, step forward, and invite the world to see what you've created.

Prepare yourself to stay focused and determined, like a treasure hunter ready to strike gold. This chapter will guide you in launching your new business with confidence and impact.

By the end, you'll engage in self-reflection and be ready to make your mark.

The Art of Launching

Look at launching your new business as if you're a musician sharing a beautiful new song for the first time, a song that resonates with emotions and tell a story. Similarly, it's your chance to introduce your business to the world, capturing the hearts of those who hear it and inspiring them to become part of your journey. This is more than just unlocking a door or putting up a "We're Open" sign outside; it's about inviting others into a world you've created with your dreams, passion, and hard work. You're encouraging them not just to buy, but to connect, to feel, and to be part of something special.

When preparing for this moment, it's important to have everything just right. Just as an artist fine-tunes every detail of a performance, every part of your business should work together smoothly. The colors, the setup, even the smallest details all work together to create something inviting and memorable. The goal isn't only to be seen but also to capture interest and grab attention. You want people to walk in and feel something special that says, "This is different."

There's a special power in the first impression. It's like setting a stage, inviting people to see something fresh and unique. Here, you get to show the personality of your business. How do you want people to feel when they hear your brand name? Warm, welcomed, excited? This is your chance to shape that feeling. Every part of your launch, from the way you greet your first visitors to the look of your brand, should reflect who you are and what you stand for.

As you step into the center of your launch day, let it be a moment that everyone remembers. There's magic in sharing something you've created with others, especially when it resonates with them. You want people to leave feeling inspired, maybe even a little surprised, wanting to come back and bring others with them. Let this launch leave a deep, lasting impression, one that builds loyalty, excitement, and a sense of connection that grows stronger each time they think of you.

Starting a business is not only about earning money, it's also about offering something that matters. When you launch, share it in a way that makes people feel something, that makes them smile, that maybe even makes them say, "I've found my place here." That's the art of a memorable launch.

Ways to Announce Your Launch Day

Launch day is a big moment, isn't it? After all those hours spent planning, dreaming, and maybe even worrying, it's finally here. The day your business comes alive! This isn't just any day; it's the first chapter in your story as an entrepreneur. So how do you let the world know about it? There are many ways, each bringing its own excitement and style.

What about throwing a party? Not just any party, but one that feels like a celebration of your dreams. This kind of event brings people together: friends, family, other business owners, and even some new faces who just heard about your venture. This is your chance to talk to people about why you started this journey, to hear them cheer you on, and to watch them smile as they see what you've been working so hard for. Giving a little speech might seem scary, but it's worth it. Sharing your story makes people feel connected, and who knows? It could be the start of lifelong friendships or loyal customers.

Of course, if parties aren't your style, there's always the power of advertising. Traditional ads, like those on TV or the radio, can be surprisingly effective. Let's say someone is watching their favorite show, and suddenly your business appears on the screen! That quick moment grabs attention. It feels like your new business just popped up to say, "Hey, I'm here! Come check me out!" Now, you've caught their eye, and that's the first step to building awareness. However, traditional ads can be surprisingly effective, but they're just the beginning.

The online world offers endless possibilities! Platforms like Facebook, Instagram, and Twitter make it easy to reach people. It's a place where you can share what you're doing behind the scenes, maybe post a few sneak peeks of your products, or give a countdown to the launch. Each post builds excitement, and it's like creating a little community of people who are excited with you. Some might comment, some will share, and with each click, word about your business spreads.

Here's another idea: hold a contest or a giveaway! People love a chance to win, and it's a fun way to get them involved. They'll spread the word for you, tagging friends and sharing posts, making your launch even bigger without you having to shout too loud. Everyone likes a good win, right? And it makes your business feel like a gift to the community even before the doors are officially open.

For a more serious tone, consider sending out a press release. Yes, it sounds fancy, but it's a simple way to reach newspapers, blogs, and even TV stations. A journalist might see your press release and think, "This is a story worth telling!" Imagine opening the newspaper or scrolling a news site and seeing your business as a featured story. It's more than just an ad; it's a story, your story, being shared with the world.

Every step, from a party to a press release, adds a little extra joy to your launch day. And remember, no matter how you choose to announce it, this day is all about you and the journey you've begun. So make it fun, make it memorable, and let everyone feel the joy you've put into your new business.

Make Your First Impression Matter

Opening your business for the first time is more than just unlocking a door. It's like introducing the world to a little piece of your heart and mind. You've spent days, maybe even months, bringing this dream to life, and now it's ready to make a big, beautiful impact. This isn't just about showing what you have to sell; it's about creating a place where people feel excited to be. The goal is to make everyone feel so welcomed and appreciated that they'll want to return whenever they can.

When a customer steps inside, you want them to feel like they've entered a special place where every detail says, "Welcome, you belong here." A big, friendly smile and a warm greeting make them feel comfortable right from the start. The space should be filled with a welcoming atmosphere, perhaps with some cheerful music in the background and a layout that lets them move around freely. A clean, inviting environment shows that every part of this place is made with care. And if you have a place where they can sit and relax for a moment, it gives them even more reason to stay and enjoy. They're not just visiting a store; they're stepping into a new favorite place.

Preparation is the secret key behind that unforgettable first impression. The kind of "wow" where everything flows so smoothly that customers can't help but be impressed. Make sure your products are ready and waiting for customers, because nothing shows "we care" like being prepared. If someone comes in looking for something, make sure it's right there, ready for them. Small touches, like having business cards they can take or brochures with more information, add that extra something that stays with them long after they leave. And if you have a team, make sure they're excited and ready to go. An organized, confident team can give customers that wonderful feeling of being in the right place at the right time.

There's something magical about a friendly conversation. A few words exchanged with customers, whether it's about their day, their interests, or just a simple greeting, helps build trust. The connection you make in those few moments can create loyalty, the kind of loyalty that keeps people returning. And when you listen, genuinely listen, they feel seen. Even a small thank you, a word of appreciation, or a friendly nod can create a wonderful memory. It's not just about transactions; it's about creating meaningful interactions.

Before they leave, let them know you want their thoughts. A little feedback, a suggestion, a quick "what did you think?" is your golden opportunity to show them how much you care about making this place the best it can be. And here's the magic: when they see you're open to their ideas, they know you're not just here to sell but to make this a place that truly works for them. So every step they take, every impression they leave with, keeps them coming back, keeps them smiling, and keeps that first impression lasting and powerful.

The Art of Attracting Customers

Attracting customers to a business is an art, and it involves making your business stand out in a way that captures attention and invites people in. When you open your doors, you want people to feel excited and happy to step inside. One good way to bring in more customers is by offering special deals, like discounts and promotions. These deals are little surprises that can catch people's attention, making them want to stop and check out what you have to offer. A nice discount might just be the reason someone decides to walk in, look around, and want to visit again.

Understanding what your customers like is like knowing what makes a friend happy. When you know what they're interested in, it's easier to create deals that they'll love. If you have a furniture store, for instance, you might notice that people love your comfortable sofas. Why not offer a discount on some of your best pieces or start a program where loyal customers can earn rewards? Deals like these make people feel valued, and they're more likely to return for that warm, friendly feeling.

Once you've planned your deals, it's important to make them stand out. How you show off your offers matters a lot! Bright signs outside your store can catch the eye of people passing by. Or maybe you could post online with fun photos of your items and clear details about the deals. You might even try a short sale that lasts just for one day, giving people a reason to hurry in. Bundle deals are also a great idea: offer a package of items at a special price so customers feel they're getting a great deal. These small touches make shopping more enjoyable, turning a quick visit into an exciting experience.

Now that you have your promotions ready, it's time to spread the word. Social media posts are a great way to let people know about your deals, especially if they're fun and easy to share. Friendly emails are also helpful, keeping your customers updated on what's new. When customers are in your store, make sure they can easily see signs about the deals. You might even offer a small discount to anyone who brings a friend along. Watching friends come in together and smile as they shop is a sure sign that you're doing something right.

Finally, take a moment to look back and see how your promotions did. Did more people come in? Were they excited about the deals? Reflecting on these questions can be rewarding. You might find yourself smiling as you remember how the store was busier than usual or how someone found exactly what they wanted. This is the time to think about what worked well so you can make your next promotions even better. Each effort you put into these promotions is a step toward a successful business filled with happy customers.

Understand Your Performance

Starting your own business is purely stepping into a dream you've built with your own hands. It's a journey filled with exciting moments that make you proud of all you've done. Each effort you've put in has brought you here, and now it's your chance to pause and truly appreciate what you've created. Take a moment to reflect and let the pride you feel wash over you, because what you're doing is something special, and it deserves to be celebrated.

As you stand here, reflecting on what you've built, it's only natural to want to know how things are really going. Just like a map helps guide you on a journey, understanding your business's performance becomes your guide. Knowing what's working gives you the motivation to keep going, and identifying any challenges early on means you can address them with confidence. Instead of wondering, you now have a clear view of the path your success is taking.

In the early days, paying attention to progress can be seen as checking the weather before going out. It helps to be aware of what's going on, so you're prepared and not caught by surprise. When you set clear goals, whether it's gaining a certain number of customers or reaching a milestone in sales, you give yourself something to celebrate. Goals are like markers along the way, reminding you that every step you take brings you closer to something bigger.

Your progress isn't hidden away in complicated reports; it's right there in front of you through something called Key Performance Indicators, or KPIs. These numbers don't need to be complicated; they're simply there to show how things are going. Are more people finding your business? Are your sales improving? These indicators give you clear signs of where you're doing well.

If you're wondering how to start using KPIs, you can begin by looking at your sales data, customer feedback, or website traffic. These are all great places to find the information that will help you track your progress and make adjustments when needed. KPIs give you the valuable insights that show you where you're on track and where you might need to make a change.

The heart of your business is the people who come in, who take a chance on your product or service, and who leave with a smile. Your customers are like trusted companions on your journey, and getting their feedback provides a secret key to success. A simple question, a moment of listening, and suddenly, they're sharing their experiences. Every bit of feedback they offer is a gift, showing you what they love and what might need a little extra care.

And let's not overlook your sales data; those numbers reveal the full view of your success. By keeping an eye on them, you begin to notice important trends. Is there something people can't get enough of? Are there specific times when business is busiest? These are signals that can guide your next move, whether it's adjusting your stock or changing your marketing approach.

As you keep your focus on these areas, you'll find your way to a deeper understanding of how well you're doing.

Face Surprises with Confidence

Wow, the day has finally arrived! After all the long wait, today is the launch you've been looking forward to. The excitement is everywhere, and the feeling of waiting for this moment is so exciting. But here's the surprise: things might not go exactly as planned, and some unexpected challenges could start sneaking in. Even with all the preparation, small issues have a way of showing up. These moments may feel like small bumps, but how you handle them can make all the difference in whether they slow you down or turn into something that drives you forward.

When surprises show up, staying calm is your superpower. You've got this. Challenges don't come to break you; they're actually new opportunities for learning, improvement, and innovation. A delay, a small problem, or a minor issue are all just life's way of encouraging you to learn and grow. When a technical problem arises, instead of letting panic take over, smile and approach it with a clear mind. Helping customers with a calm and confident attitude works wonders. Not only will they feel cared for, but your calmness will spread to your team, creating a focused and relaxed atmosphere for everyone.

Now, even the best surprises don't feel too surprising when you're a little prepared. You can expect common challenges and trust that you'll handle them as they come. So, if the audience turns out to be larger than expected, make sure you have enough stock and a comfortable waiting area where guests can relax with some refreshments. A little bit of thoughtfulness here makes a big difference. Every smile you bring to someone waiting reminds them that this launch is all about creating something special for them and with them.

And here's the key to making this launch truly amazing: the bond with your team. Begin the day with everyone together, a quick check-in to lift morale and make sure everyone's feeling good about the plan. This simple moment goes a long way. Throughout the day, keep those team connections strong with quick, supportive words or a helping hand. When people feel valued, their energy flows into everything they do, making your customers feel that much more welcome and cared for. Let each person's ideas and strengths shine. It makes everything smoother and creates a positive flow that everyone can follow.

Flexibility is one of your most valuable tools, especially on a big day. When things don't go as planned, staying calm and open to finding solutions can turn a challenge into an opportunity. If a delivery is delayed or something unexpected happens, instead of panicking, offer a similar product or a small discount. This shows your customers that you're not only prepared but that you care about their experience. By making these adjustments, you let people know they're in good hands, building trust and leaving them with the reassurance that you are focused on making things right for them.

As you face each moment, let the experience fill you with pride. The mix of calm, care, and adaptability you bring today is the real magic behind this launch. Every surprise you overcome makes the day richer and more memorable. The happiness in the room reflects all the joy, effort, and creativity you've poured into making this day a success for everyone involved.

Self-Reflection

Next, move on to the following questions to assess your readiness for launching your dream business.

Questions	My Answer
1. How do I feel about my business launch?	

2. How will I announce my business?	
3. What's one great way to celebrate my business launch?	
4. What promotions will I offer?	
5. What should I check to measure my business's success?	
6. Why is it important to plan details before my launch?	
7. How does customer feedback help after the launch?	
8. How can social media support my launch?	
9. Why should I greet customers warmly on launch day?	
10. How can I handle challenges calmly on launch day?	

Figure 10.1: Self-Assessment Questions

Conclusion

As we reach the end of *The Entrepreneur's Tickets: A Step-By-Step Guide to Building Your Dream Business*, it's important to reflect on the journey we've taken together. Starting this book is like beginning an exciting adventure, filled with possibilities and new discoveries. Just as every great journey starts with a single step, so too does your entrepreneurial path begin with the insights and tools you've gathered here.

Each ticket in this book has provided you with valuable wisdom to navigate various challenges in building your dream business. Think of each ticket as a gateway to new experiences and lessons, designed to empower you on your journey. Just as a ticket to an exclusive event grants you access to unforgettable experiences, the knowledge you've gained here opens doors to remarkable opportunities. So take this knowledge to heart, use it wisely, and remember that each experience will help guide you on your path.

As you move forward, let the memories of your journey fill you with happiness and inspiration. Your adventure is just starting, and with each step, you'll find new chances to grow and succeed. So get ready, believe in yourself, and prepare to create the business of your dreams!

Conquer Challenges and Celebrate Your Wins!

When starting your dream business, you're taking on an exciting journey. There will be ups and downs that test your strength. You might worry about funds, wonder how to compete, or question your choices. But remember, each challenge is a chance to learn and grow. These tough times help you become the entrepreneur you want to be. Many successful entrepreneurs have faced similar problems and came out stronger.

When things get tough, take a moment to celebrate your successes, no matter how small. Did you finish your launch? Make your first sale? Each step forward matters! Celebrating these moments keeps your spirits up and reminds you that you are making progress. These little wins boost your confidence and bring you closer to your goals.

As you start this journey, believe in your skills and passion. See challenges as opportunities to learn, and celebrate every win. Stay focused on your goals and keep your dream in sight. Each step you take is part of your story, and overcoming obstacles makes your future success even better. Keep moving forward and trust that you can achieve great things. Your path may have ups and downs, but every experience will help you grow.

Stay Motivated

Staying motivated as an entrepreneur can be hard, but it's essential for success. Think of your journey as an adventure with its own highs and lows. Some days, things may seem slow, and the challenges might feel big. In those times, remember why you started. Did you want freedom? To help others? Or to create something lasting? Keeping your purpose in mind helps you get through tough times.

Make sure to wake up every day with clear goals in mind. To keep that vision alive, create a daily routine that works for you. This routine helps you stay organized and focused. Surround yourself with positive people who support you. Friends, mentors, and fellow entrepreneurs can inspire you and lift your spirits.

Set small, achievable goals along the way. Think of these goals as little victories. When you reach them, you'll see real progress, which keeps you motivated. Each small success boosts your confidence and brings you closer to your big dreams.

Remember, everyone faces setbacks. When challenges come, try to see them as temporary. Like a rainstorm that eventually ends, tough times will pass. Trust in your strength to overcome them.

Take a deep breath, learn from what happened, and keep moving forward.

Cook Up Your Success

Success is not just about avoiding mistakes. It's about learning from them and getting better each time. Think of it like cooking. When you try a new recipe, it may not turn out great at first. But with practice and a little creativity, you can make a tasty dish that you will be proud to share.

The world is full of chances, just like a kitchen full of ingredients. Suppose you're in your kitchen with fresh vegetables, spices, and other items. Each ingredient represents an opportunity for you to create something special. Just like in cooking, where you mix flavors to find what works best, you can try different ideas and approaches in business. Remember, some recipes take time to perfect, and your business ideas might need a few tries before they succeed. That's okay! Each attempt teaches you something valuable for the next time.

Stay flexible and open to change. The business world is always changing, and being adaptable is very important. Surround yourself with helpful people, like mentors and friends who can guide you. Each person you meet and every new skill you learn will help you on your journey to success.

As you build your business, remember you have a chance to help others. Your success can inspire those around you and help your community grow. Think of a bridge: when it's strong, it connects two sides and helps people cross from one place to another. By helping others, you not only make your business stronger but also create chances for growth in your community.

References

Dweck, C. S. (2007). *Mindset: The new psychology of success.* Ballantine Books.

Neck, H. M., Neck, C. P., & Murray, E. L. (2016). *Entrepreneurship: The practice and mindset.* Sage Publications.

Workie, B., Chane, M., Mohammed, M., & Birhanu, T. (2019). *Entrepreneurship.* Ministry of Science and Higher Education of Ethiopia.

United Republic of Tanzania. (2019). *The Tax Administration Act [Principal legislation], Revised edition. Attorney General*

United Republic of Tanzania. (2023). *The Investment Act [Principal legislation], Revised edition. Attorney General*

United Republic of Tanzania. (1995). *The Immigration Act. Attorney General*

United Republic of Tanzania. *The Employment and Labour Relations Act. Attorney General*

United Republic of Tanzania. (2019). *The Income Tax Act [Principal legislation], Revised edition. Attorney General*

United Republic of Tanzania. (2019). *The Value Added Tax Act [Principal legislation], Revised edition. Attorney General*

United Republic of Tanzania. (2002). *The Companies Act, Revised edition. Attorney General*

United Republic of Tanzania. (2024). *Taxes and duties at a glance.* Tanzania Revenue Authority.

About the Author

Omary S. Omary was born into a poor family on Tandale Street in Dar Es Salaam, Tanzania with a dream: to one day become one of the leading experts who empower entrepreneurs and pave their way to success. Growing up in a challenging life inspired him to work hard and become the skilled professional he is today.

Omary holds a Bachelor's degree in Banking and Finance from IFM (Dar), a Postgraduate Diploma in Taxation from ITA (Dar), and an MBA in Corporate Management from IAA (Arusha). Currently, he's pursuing ACCA (UK), aiming to reach new heights and continually advance in his field, embracing lifelong learning.

Despite applying for many jobs and not finding success in employment, Omary didn't give up. This led him to start his own journey as an independent consultant in 2018, right after earning his degree this year. He has since helped many small and large entrepreneurs navigate tax issues, regulatory compliance, and advisory services for starting, running, and growing their businesses.

Today, Omary is more than just an author; he's a registered and certified tax consultant and business expert. He is also the proud founder of Tax Digital Lamp, a consulting company known for its innovative approach.

You can connect with him on:
- Linkedin: *(Search for Omary S. Omary)*.
- Facebook: *(Search for Omary S. Omary)*.
- Instagram: *(Search for omaryomarybooks)*.